CYCLES

The Second Year

CYCLES

The Second Year

God's Word in the Modern World

EDITED BY
LOUIS M. SAVARY, S. J.

REGINA PRESS
New York
1972

Cycles: The Second Year
Copyright © 1972 by Max Odorff, Inc.
225 East 57th St., New York, N. Y. 10022

Library of Congress Catalog Card Number: 72–87358

Printed in the United States of America

PREFACE

Today, more and more people are turning away from the material-
ism of their lives to search for spiritual values. Man seeks God and
eventually finds that God is in search of man. He speaks to us
through all his creation; the heavens and the earth proclaim his
presence. His is also the language of steel and concrete, of
crowded cities and busy roads. His voice is in all the yearning and
striving of mankind towards a deeper, more human life.

Cycles offers themes for reflection on God's presence to man.
Scripture readings find new echoes in contemporary photographs
and texts, which show the perennial freshness of God's word in
the modern world.

ACKNOWLEDGEMENTS

Many of the works from which selections herein are taken are protected by copyright, and may not be reproduced in any form without the consent of the authors, their publishers, or their agents. Every effort has been made to trace the ownership of all selections in this book and to obtain the necessary authorization for their use. If any errors or omissions have occurred in this regard, corrections will be made in all future editions of this book.

Grateful acknowledgement is made to: Abingdon Press for selections by W. A. Smart from *Contemporary Thinking About Jesus*, ed. Thomas S. Kepler, copyright © 1944 Whitmore & Stone, and John J. Vincent from *Secular Christ*, copyright © 1968 John J. Vincent; Argus Communications for selections by Norbert M. Luyten from *Death to Life*, copyright © 1968 Argus Communications; Association Press for selections by Roger Hazelton and Revel L. Howe from *New Frontiers of Christianity*, ed. Ralph Raughley, Jr., copyright © 1962 NB/YMCA; Beacon Press for selections by Albert Schweitzer from *The Psychiatric Study of Jesus*, copyright © 1948 Beacon Press; Chelsea House Publishers for selection by Billy Sunday from *Billy Sunday Speaks*, copyright © 1970 Chelsea House Publishers; Dimension Books, Inc. for selections by Ladislas M. Orsy from *The Lord of Confusion*, © 1970 Ladislas M. Orsy, S.J.; Dodd, Mead & Co. for selections by G. K. Chesterton from *Orthodoxy*, copyright © 1947 Dodd, Mead & Co.; Doubleday & Company, Inc. for selections by Bernhard Alfrink from *Infallible? An Inquiry*, by Hans Küng, copyright © 1966 Doubleday & Company, Inc., G. K. Chesterton from *The Real Jesus* by Louis Cassels copyright © 1968 Louis Cassels, and Helen Keller from *My Religion*, copyright © 1927 The Swedenborg Foundation; Farrar, Straus & Giroux, Inc. for selections by Martin D'Arcy from *The Meaning and Matter of History*, copyright © 1959 Farrar, Straus & Giroux, Inc., and Flannery O'Connor from *The Violent Bear It Away*, copyright © 1955, 1960 Flannery O'Connor; Fortress Press for selection by Dietrich Bonhoeffer from *World Come of Age*, ed. R. Gregor Smith, copyright © 1967 Fortress Press; Franciscan Herald Press for selections by Kevin O'Sullivan from *The Sunday Readings*, copyright © 1971 Rev. Kevin O'Sullivan; Harper & Row, Publishers for selections by Karl Barth from *The Word of God and The Word of Man*, copyright © 1957 Harper & Row, Publishers, Dietrich Bonhoeffer from *Christ the Center*, copyright © 1966 Harper & Row, Publishers, Pierre Teilhard de Chardin from *The Divine Milieu*, copyright © 1960 Harper & Row, Publishers, and *Writings in Time of War*, copyright © 1968 Harper & Row, Publishers, C. H. Dodd from *The Authority of the Bible*, copyright © 1929 Harper & Row, Publishers, by Mircea

(*Acknowledgments continued on page 270*)

CONTENTS

ADVENT
AND
CHRISTMAS

Waiting for the Lord

Israel's response to God
introduced a new category
into religious experience:
the category of *faith*.
It must not be forgotten
that, if Abraham's faith can be defined
as 'for God everything is possible,'
the faith of Christianity implies
that everything is also possible for man . . .
Faith in this context, as in many others,
means absolute emancipation . . .
and hence the highest freedom
that man can imagine:
freedom to intervene
even in the . . . constitution of the universe.
It is, consequently, a pre-eminently creative freedom.
Mircea Eliade

Jesus said to his disciples:
"Be constantly on the watch!
Stay awake! You do not know
when the appointed time will come . . .
You do not know
when the master of the house is coming,
whether at dusk, at midnight,
when the cock crows, or at early dawn.
Do not let him come suddenly
and catch you asleep.
What I say to you, I say to all:
Be on guard!"
Mark 13:33, 35–37

You, Lord are our father,
our redeemer you are named forever.
Why do you let us wander, O Lord, from your ways,
and harden our hearts so that we fear you not?
Return for the sake of your servants,
the tribes of your heritage.
Oh, that you would rend the heavens
and come down,
with the mountains quaking before you.

Isaiah 63:16–17, 19

We believe, Lord, in your word;
we will try to follow and live it.
Now we hear its echo reverberating
in the souls of the men of our century.
It seems to tell us:
Blessed are we, if in poverty of spirit
we learn to free ourselves
from false confidence in material things
and to place our chief desires
in spiritual and religious goods,
treating the poor with respect and love
as brothers and living images of Christ.

Pope Paul VI

The witness I bore to Christ
has been so confirmed among you
that you lack no spiritual gift
as you wait for the revelation
of our Lord Jesus Christ.
He will strengthen you to the end,
so that you will be blameless
on the day of our Lord Jesus Christ.
God is faithful,
and it was he who called you
to fellowship with his Son,
Jesus Christ our Lord.

1 Corinthians 1:6–9

Preparing Your Way

Each individual Christian,
businessman, citizen,
needs to follow in his steps
along the path of personal sacrifice
for him.
There is not a different path today
from that of Jesus' own times.
It is the same path.
The call is for a new discipleship,
a new following of Jesus,
more like the early, simple,
apostolic Christianity
when the disciples left all
and literally followed the Master.
Nothing but a discipleship of this kind
can face the destructive selfishness of the age,
with any hope of overcoming it.

Charles M. Sheldon

Instead of taking flight from history,
the people of Israel . . .
turned toward Yahweh for *salvation*:
a salvation that was strangely already present
and yet to be fully realized in the future.
God was present in the midst of his people
in his Word, but he was not present fully,
definitively and ultimately.
The full realization of Yahweh's presence
was to be found only in the future.

Leon McKenzie

In the desert prepare the way of the Lord!
Make straight in the wasteland
a highway for our God!
Every valley shall be filled in,
every mountain and hill shall be made low;
The rugged land shall be made a plain,
the rough country, a broad valley.
Then the glory of the Lord shall be revealed,
and all mankind shall see it together;
for the mouth of the Lord has spoken.

Isaiah 40:3–5

In the Lord's eyes,
one day is as a thousand years
and a thousand years are as a day.
The Lord does not delay in keeping his promise—
though some consider it "delay."
Rather, he shows you generous patience,
since he wants none to perish
but all to come to repentance . . .
What we await are new heavens
and a new earth
where, according to his promise,
the justice of God will reside.
So, beloved, while waiting for this,
make every effort to be found
without stain or defilement,
and at peace in his sight.

2 Peter 3:8–9, 13–14

In Isaiah the prophet, it is written:
"I send my messenger before you
to prepare your way:
a herald's voice in the desert, crying,
'Make ready the way of the Lord,
clear him a straight path.' "
Thus it was that John the Baptizer
appeared in the desert
proclaiming a baptism of repentance
which led to the forgiveness of sins . . .
The theme of his preaching was:
"One more powerful than I is to come after me.
I am not fit to stoop and untie his sandal straps.
I have baptized you in water;
he will baptize you in the Holy Spirit."

Mark 1:2–4, 7–8

The Spirit of the Lord

I don't know Who—or what—
put the question,
I don't know when it was put.
I don't even remember answering.
But at some moment I did answer *Yes*
to Someone—or Something—
and from that hour
I was certain that existence is meaningful
and that, therefore,
my life, in self-surrender,
had a goal.

Dag Hammarskjöld

Do not stifle the spirit.
Do not despise prophecies.
Test everything; retain what is good.
Avoid any semblance of evil.
May the God of peace
make you perfect in holiness.
May you be preserved whole and entire,
spirit, soul, and body,
irreproachable at the coming
of our Lord Jesus Christ.

1 Thessalonians 5:19–23

There was a man named John sent by God,
who came as a witness
to testify to the light,
so that through him
all men might believe—
but only to testify to the light,
for he himself was not the light.

John 1:6–8

The spirit of the Lord God is upon me,
because the Lord has anointed me;
He has sent me to bring glad tidings to the lowly,
to heal the brokenhearted,
To proclaim liberty to the captives
and release to the prisoners,
To announce a year of favor from the Lord.

Isaiah 61:1–2

The Spirit, without moving,
is swifter than the mind;
the senses cannot reach him:
he is ever beyond them.
Standing still, he overtakes those who run.
To the ocean of his being,
the spirit of life leads the streams of action.

He moves, and he moves not.
He is far, and he is near.
He is within all, and he is outside all.

Isa Upanishad

The Hidden Mystery

I sought to find my way between
the problem of human life on the one hand
and the content of the Bible on the other.
As a minister I wanted to speak to the *people*
in the infinite contradiction of their life,
but to speak the no less infinite
message of the Bible,
which was as much of a riddle as life.

Karl Barth

" 'It was I who took you from the pasture
and from the care of the flock
to be commander of my people Israel.
I have been with you wherever you went,
and I have destroyed all your enemies before you.
And I will make you famous
like the great ones of the earth.
I will fix a place for my people Israel;
I will plant them so that they may dwell
in their place without further disturbance.' "

2 Samuel 7:8–10

Goodness does not really exist
until it exists in a life,
just as color does not exist
except as it exists in colored objects.
There is no such thing as love
except as someone actually feels love
for someone else.
Until then it is merely an abstraction . . .
and so God's great idea, his Word,
became flesh and dwelt among us.

When we see this Word of God incarnate
we see what God meant,
for he is the final commentary
on everything that he said.

W. A. Smart

"Do not fear, Mary.
You have found favor with God.
You shall conceive and bear a son
and give him the name Jesus.
Great will be his dignity
and he will be called Son of the Most High.
The Lord God will give him
the throne of David his father.
He will rule over the house of Jacob forever
and his reign will be without end . . .
the holy offspring to be born
will be called Son of God."

Luke 1:30–33, 35

To him who is able to strengthen you
in the gospel which I proclaim
when I preach Jesus Christ,
the gospel which reveals the mystery
hidden for many ages
but now manifested
through the writings of the prophets,
and, at the command of the eternal God,
made known to all the Gentiles
that they may believe and obey—
to him . . . may glory be given
through Jesus Christ unto endless ages. Amen.

Romans 16:25–26

Christmas: Our Blessed Hope

Through the soul of the world,
and through that soul alone
the Word, becoming incarnate in the universe,
has been able to establish
a vital, immediate, relationship
with each one of the animate elements
that make up the cosmos.

Through that soul, accordingly,
and for all time,
the human-divine influence of Christ
encompasses us, penetrates us,
identifies itself with all the forces of our growth
as individuals and as a social whole.

Pierre Teilhard de Chardin

We await our blessed hope,
the appearing of the glory of the great God
and of our Savior Christ Jesus.
It was he who sacrificed himself for us,
to redeem us from all unrighteousness
and to cleanse for himself
a people of his own,
eager to do what is right.

Titus 2:13–14

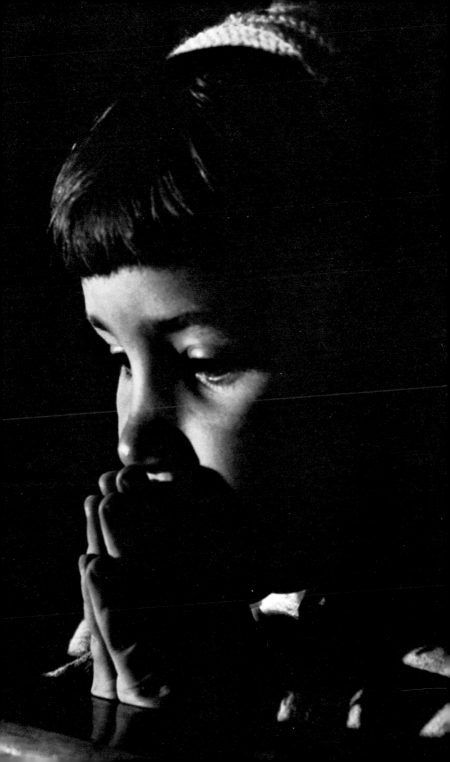

A child is born to us, a son is given us;
upon his shoulder dominion rests.
They name him Wonder-Counselor, God-Hero,
Father-Forever, Prince of Peace.
His dominion is vast
and forever peaceful.

Isaiah 9:5–6

Joseph went from the town
of Nazareth in Galilee to Judea,
to David's town of Bethlehem—
because he was of the house and lineage of David—
to register with Mary, his espoused wife,
who was with child.
While they were there
the days of her confinement were completed.
She gave birth to her first-born son
and wrapped him in swaddling clothes
and laid him in a manger,
because there was no room for them
in the place where travelers lodged.

Luke 2:4–7

I went with them to see for myself
and I found a woman in labor
amongst those round the brazier
and her baby was born
under the winter stars that night.
"There was no room for them at the inn" . . .
and so, on a winter night in Bethlehem,
nearly two thousand years ago,
the Son of God had entered his world
in the bleak and barren shelter of a stable.
It has come back to me again and again
in the richest city of the Southern Hemisphere
just how easily man can reject
the Christ he proclaims to worship.

Trevor Huddleston

A Bond of Union

My son, take care of your father when he is old;
grieve him not as long as he lives.
Even if his mind fail, be considerate with him;
revile him not in the fullness of your strength.
For kindness to a father will not be forgotten . . .

Sirach 3:12–14

There lived in Jerusalem at the time
a certain man named Simeon.
He was just and pious,
and awaited the consolation of Israel,
and the Holy Spirit was upon him.
It was revealed to him by the Holy Spirit
that he would not experience death
until he had seen the Anointed of the Lord.
He came to the temple now,
inspired by the Spirit;
and when the parents brought in the child Jesus
to perform for him the customary ritual of the law,
he took him in his arms
and blessed God in these words:
"Now, Master, you can dismiss your servant in peace;
you have fulfilled your word.
For my eyes have witnessed your saving deed
displayed for all the peoples to see:
A revealing light to the Gentiles,
the glory of your people Israel."

Luke 2:25–32

As the world grows closer to God,
as the world is humbled,
as the world is purified,
it will come to a deeper knowledge
and an eventual understanding
of that mystery of unity and diversity
which is his own life
and which is the expression, the bond,
of his own personal relation
with the Savior himself.

John LaFarge

Even among men, gratitude creates
an intimate communion.
Gratitude is ultimately such a strong bond
that nothing can break it.
How much more so with God.
Because we fail to give thanks,
we do not have communion with him . . .
To pray means first to give thanks,
and many never achieve
true communion with him in their prayers
because they do not begin with thanksgiving.

Albert Schweitzer

Dedicate yourselves to thankfulness.
Let the word of Christ, rich as it is, dwell in you.
In wisdom made perfect,
instruct and admonish one another.
Sing gratefully to God from your hearts
in psalms, hymns, and inspired songs.
Whatever you do,
whether in speech or in action,
do it in the name of the Lord Jesus.
Give thanks to God the Father through him.

Colossians 3:15–17

The Spirit of Sonship

The shepherds went in haste to Bethlehem
and found Mary and Joseph,
and the baby lying in the manger;
once they saw, they understood
what had been told them concerning this child.
All who heard of it were astonished
at the report given them by the shepherds . . .
The shepherds returned,
glorifying and praising God
for all they had heard and seen,
in accord with what had been told them.

Luke 2:16–18, 20

"The Lord bless you and keep you!
The Lord let his face shine upon you,
and be gracious to you!
The Lord look upon you kindly
and give you peace!"

Numbers 6:24–26

The proof that you are sons
is the fact that God has sent forth
into our hearts the spirit of his Son,
which cries out "Abba!" ("Father!").
You are no longer a slave but a son!
And the fact that you are a son
makes you an heir, by God's design.

                              Galatians 4:6–7

Thanks be to Thee,
my Joy and my Glory
and my Hope and my God:
thanks be to Thee for Thy gifts:
but do Thou preserve them in me,
Thus Thou wilt preserve me,
and the things Thou has given me
will increase and be made perfect,
and I shall be with Thee:
because even that I exist is Thy gift.

                              St. Augustine

I caught this morning morning's minion, king-
        dom of daylight's dauphin, dapple-dawn-drawn Falcon,
            in his riding
        Of the rolling level underneath him steady air, and striding
High there, how he rung upon the rein of a wimpling wing
In his ecstasy! then off, off forth on swing,
        As a skate's heel sweeps smooth on a bow-bend;
            the hurl and gliding
        Rebuffed the big wind. My heart in hiding
Stirred for a bird,—the achieve of, the mastery
            of the thing!

Brute beauty and valour and act, oh, air, pride, plume here
        Buckle! And the fire that breaks from thee then,
            a billion
Times told lovelier, more dangerous, O my chevalier!

        No wonder of it: shéer plód makes plough down sillion
Shine, and blue-bleak embers, ah my dear,
        Fall, gall themselves, and gash gold-vermilion.
                                Gerard Manley Hopkins
                                    The Windhover:
                                    To Christ our Lord

The Innermost Vision

By love he knows me in truth,
who I am and what I am.
And when he knows me in truth
he enters into my Being.

Bhagavad Gita 18.55

May the God of our Lord Jesus Christ,
the Father of glory,
grant you a spirit of wisdom and insight
to know him clearly.
May he enlighten your innermost vision
that you may know the great hope
to which he has called you,
the wealth of his glorious heritage
to be distributed among the members of the church.

Ephesians 1:17–18

If the Church
has the spirit of Jesus
there is room in her
for every form
of Christian piety,
even for that which claims
unrestricted liberty.

Albert Schweitzer

The Word became flesh
and made his dwelling among us,
and we have seen his glory:
the glory of an only Son
coming from the Father,
filled with enduring love . . .
Of his fullness
we have all had a share—
love following upon love.

John 1:14, 16

Before all ages,
in the beginning,
he created me,
and through all ages
I shall not cease to be.

Sirach 24:8

Bringing Mankind Together

Astrologers from the east arrived one day
in Jerusalem inquiring,
"Where is the newborn king of the Jews?
We observed his star at its rising
and have come to pay him homage." . . .
After their audience with the king, they set out.
The star which they had observed at its rising
went ahead of them until it came to a standstill
over the place where the child was.
They were overjoyed at seeing the star,
and on entering the house,
found the child with Mary his mother.
They prostrated themselves and did him homage.
Then they opened their coffers
and presented him with gifts
of gold, frankincense, and myrrh.

Matthew 2:1–2, 9–11

Then shall you be radiant at what you see,
your heart shall throb and overflow.
For the riches of the sea
shall be emptied out before you,
the wealth of nations shall be brought to you.
Caravans of camels shall fill you,
dromedaries from Midian and Ephah;
All from Sheba shall come
bearing gold and frankincense,
and proclaiming the praises of the Lord.

Isaiah 60:5–6

Anyone who is prepared to come to terms
with schism in the Church,
anyone capable of being at ease with it,
anyone to whom the sight of the obvious faults
and errors in the other side,
and hence their responsibility for it,
provides a reason for being tranquil about it,
may be a good, loyal believer in some sense
that belongs to his particular denomination—
a good Roman or Calvinist or Orthodox or Baptist—
but he must not think that he can possibly
be a good Christian.

Karl Barth

We have carried on the debate
with the utmost frankness
and given others the opportunity,
as far as they wanted,
to be witnesses of what we were doing
and to be drawn into it.
Once again, not as propaganda,
but only to render a service.
For what we discussed were really
not our questions alone.
No one can dispose of the message of the Lord
as of an exclusive possession.
We shall have to experience it
always as a challenge
and thus for ourselves too
occasionally as a painful message.
In this way too we hope to contribute something
to the reconciliation of the Churches.

Bernhard Alfrink

That same freedom in civil society
which the Church has ever insisted upon
for herself and her members,
she now in this our age
also champions for other churches
and their members,
indeed for every human person.

Richard Cardinal Cushing

44

God's secret plan,
as I have briefly described it,
was revealed to me,
unknown to men in former ages
but now revealed by the Spirit
to the holy apostles and prophets.
It is no less than this: in Christ Jesus
the Gentiles are now co-heirs with the Jews,
members of the same body
and sharers of the promise
through the preaching of the gospel.

Ephesians 3:3, 5–6

Let us make the courageous resolution
to bring men together
instead of dividing them,
eliminate from our vocabulary and conversation
all that can hurt or wound our neighbor,
so that there may descend on our earth
a little of that peace God has promised
to men of good will.

Léon Joseph Suenens

Anointed with the Holy Spirit

Instead of looking at books and pictures
about the New Testament
I looked at the New Testament.
There I found an account, not in the least
of a person with his hair parted in the middle
or his hands clasped in appeal,
but of an extraordinary being with lips of thunder
and acts of lurid decision,
flinging down tables, casting out devils,
passing with the wild secrecy of the wind,
from mountain isolation
to a sort of dreadful demagogy;
a being who often acted like an angry god—
and always like a god.

G. K. Chesterton

Here is my servant whom I uphold,
my chosen one with whom I am pleased.
Upon whom I have put my spirit;
he shall bring forth justice to the nations,
Not crying out, not shouting,
not making his voice heard in the street.
A bruised reed he shall not break,
and a smoldering wick he shall not quench,
Until he establishes justice on the earth;
the coastlands will wait for his teaching.

Isaiah 42:1–4

Jesus came from Nazareth in Galilee,
and was baptized in the Jordan by John.
Immediately on coming up out of the water
he saw the sky rent in two
and the Spirit descending on him like a dove.
Then a voice came from the heavens:
"You are my beloved Son.
On you my favor rests."

Mark 1:9–11

Christ does not stand before us
at one time as man
and other time as God,
but as the God-Man,
as a man whose every word,
every attitude, every act,
and entire visible human being
testifies to his divinity,
and is an epiphany of God.

Dietrich von Hildebrand

"I take it you know what has been reported
all over Judea about Jesus of Nazareth,
beginning in Galilee
with the baptism John preached;
of the way God anointed him
with the Holy Spirit and power.
He went about doing good works
and healing all who were in the grip of the devil,
and God was with him."

Acts 10:36–38

THE
SEASON
OF
LENT

The Good News

As a person God gives personal life,
he makes us as persons become capable
of meeting with him and with one another.
But no limitation can come upon him
as the absolute person,
either from us
or from our relations with one another;
in fact we can dedicate to him
not merely our persons
but also our relations to one another.

Martin Buber

God said to Noah and to his sons with him:
"See, I am now establishing my covenant
with you and your descendants after you
and with every living creature
that was with you:
all the birds, and the various tame and wild animals
that were with you and came out of the ark.
I will establish my covenant with you,
that never again shall all bodily creatures
be destroyed by the waters of a flood;
there shall not be another flood
to devastate the earth."

Genesis 9:8–11

Jesus appeared in Galilee
proclaiming God's good news:
"This is the time of fulfillment.
The reign of God is at hand!
Reform your lives
and believe in the good news!"
Mark 1:14–15

We have to remark how firmly
Jesus believes in his Gospel
of God and man needing each other
and finding each other—
his "good news," as he calls it.
He bases all on his faith
in what has been called
"Man's incurable religious instinct"—
that instinct in the human heart that must have God—
and in God's response to that instinct
which he himself implanted,
and which is no accident
found here and missing there,
but a genuine God-given characteristic
of every man, whatever his temperament
or his range in emotions may be,
his swiftness or slowness of mind.
The repeated parables of seed and leaven—
the parables of vitality—
again and again suggest his faith
in his message, his conviction
that God must have man
and man must have God—
T. R. Glover

At that time [Noah's], a few persons, eight in all,
escaped in the ark through the water.
You are now saved by a baptismal bath
which corresponds to this exactly.
This baptism is no removal of physical stain,
but the pledge to God
of an irreproachable conscience
through the resurrection of Jesus Christ.

1 Peter 3:20–21

This Is My Son

Jesus took Peter, James and John
off by themselves with him
and led them up a high mountain.
He was transfigured before their eyes
and his clothes became dazzlingly white—
whiter than the work of any bleacher
could make them.
Elijah appeared to them along with Moses;
the two were in conversation with Jesus . . .
A cloud came, overshadowing them,
and out of the cloud a voice:
"This is my son, my beloved.
Listen to him."
Suddenly looking around
they no longer saw anyone with them—
only Jesus.

Mark 9:2–4, 7–8

"I swear by myself, declares the Lord,
that because you acted as you did
in not withholding from me your beloved son,
I will bless you abundantly
and make your descendants
as countless as the stars of the sky
and the sands of the seashore;
your descendants shall take possession
of the gates of their enemies,
and in your descendants
all the nations of the earth shall find blessing—
all this because you obeyed my command."

Genesis 22:16–18

The revelatory answer is meaningless
if there is no question
to which it is the answer.
Man cannot receive an answer
to a question he has not asked . . .
Any such answer would be foolishness for him,
an understandable combination of words—
as so much preaching is—
but not a revelatory experience.

Paul Tillich

It is a remarkable fact that Christ
has been able to remain
the archetypal man of Western civilization
in its transition from medieval to modern form.
The fact itself can be ascertained
from the lives of outstanding men and women
of modern times.
Its explanation is perhaps that Christ,
the mediator between God and man,
could be the prototype not only of medieval mediators,
the medieval "lords spiritual" and "lords temporal,"
but also of modern men who have no mediators.
For the mediator himself has no mediator—
Christ's own relationship to God
was an unmediated one.
Christ, especially in his passion,
can readily be taken as the prototype
both of the man who for lack of mediation
feels too close to God,
who feels that he has
"fallen into the hands of the living God,"
and of the man who for lack of mediation
feels out of touch with God,
who feels that God is silent
or absent or dead.
The words "My God, my God,
why have you forsaken me?"
which Christ uttered upon the cross,
have become meaningful to the modern man
in his unmediated existence
in a way that they could not be
to the medieval man living
in the hierarchical world of mediation.

John S. Dunne

Christ, the Power of God

The Jews sought salvation
by way of literal observance of a Law
and by obedience to the commands of a God
Who made his power manifest in miracles of glory;
the Greeks sought a salvation
to be achieved by way of the rectitude of the will
and the certitude afforded
by the natural light of reason.
What had Christianity to offer either?
Salvation by faith in Christ crucified,
that is to say a scandal to the Jews
who asked for a sign of power
and were offered the infamy of an humiliated God:
a folly to the Greeks
who sought after the intelligible,
and were offered the absurdity
of a God-man, dead on a cross
and risen again from the dead to save us.
Christianity had nothing
to oppose to the wisdom of the world
but the scandalous and impenetrable mystery of Jesus.

Étienne Gilson

Jews demand "signs"
and Greeks look for "wisdom,"
but we preach Christ crucified,
a stumbling block to Jews,
and an absurdity to Gentiles;
but to those who are called,
Jews and Greeks alike,
Christ is the power of God
and the wisdom of God.

1 Corinthians 1:22–24

God delivered all these commandments:
"I, the Lord, am your God,
who brought you out of the land of Egypt,
that place of slavery.
You shall not have other gods besides me . . .
You shall not take the name
of the Lord, your God, in vain.
For the Lord will not leave unpunished
him who takes his name in vain."

Exodus 20:1–3, 7

This eternal factor in Christ and his gospel
was present from the start.
He appealed to profundities in human nature,
which passing centuries
and changing cultures do not affect.
He did deal with the problems
presented by current Phariseeism,
legalism, nationalism,
and even with special problems
such as the Jewish system of divorce,
but his solutions had the dimension of depth,
so that they have carried over,
their truth applicable to situations
utterly different from first-century culture . . .

Jesus had a way of putting things
that time does not wear out.

Harry Emerson Fosdick

As the Jewish Passover was near,
Jesus went up to Jerusalem.
In the temple precincts he came upon people
engaging in selling oxen, sheep and doves,
and others seated changing coins.
He made a kind of whip of cords
and drove them all out of the temple area,
sheep and oxen alike,
and knocked over the money-changers' tables,
spilling their coins.
He told those who were selling doves:
"Get them out of here!
Stop turning my Father's house
into a marketplace!"

John 2:13–16

Jesus was no maker of programs,
no framer of agenda to be acted on
by individuals or assemblies
through all time to come.
Nor was he a creator
of moral or religious credenda
once for all delivered to his followers.
His religion struck its roots
more deeply into the life of the soul . . .
Opinions and deeds, to be of value,
must be the expressions of a pure heart.
Make the tree itself good
and the fruits thereof
would be of proper quality.

Shirley Jackson Case

63

God's Great Love for Us

He cannot be taught
by one who has not reached him;
and he cannot be reached
by much thinking.
The way to him
is through a Teacher who has seen him:
He is higher than the highest thoughts,
in truth above all thought.

Katha Upanishad

Jesus said to Nicodemus:
"Just as Moses lifted up the serpent in the desert,
so much the Son of Man be lifted up,
that all who believe
may have eternal life in him.
Yes, God so loved the world
that he gave his only Son,
that whoever believes in him may not die
but may have eternal life.
God did not send the Son into the world
to condemn the world,
but that the world might be saved through him."

John 3:14–17

He did not notice
that it was they
who were putting him to death,
but rather that he
was in the act
of dying for them.

St. Augustine

Early and often did the Lord,
the God of their fathers,
send his messengers to them,
for he had compassion on his people
and his dwelling place.
But they mocked the messengers of God,
despised his warnings,
and scoffed at his prophets,
until the anger of the Lord
against his people
was so inflamed that there was no remedy.
2 Chronicles 36:15–16

All human misery
comes from greed;
wretchedness of body from men's refusal
to give their goods;
wretchedness of soul from men's refusal
to give their time and their hearts.
Isabel Rivière

God is rich in mercy;
because of his great love for us
he brought us to life with Christ
when we were dead in sin.
By this favor you were saved.
Both with and in Christ Jesus he raised us up
and gave us a place in the heavens,
that in the ages to come
he might display the great wealth of his favor,
manifested by his kindness to us in Christ Jesus.
Ephesians 2:4–7

The Source of Salvation

Jesus seems to have perceived
the good lurking under the evil.
He could quench the evil
and quicken the good
by giving to the sinner
somebody to admire and to love.
He asked for service,
and put it in the place of sin.
The hatefulness of his past life
was brought vividly to the mind of the sinner
as the antithesis of his new affection
and of his loving gratitude.
It was, doubtless, often a daring method;
even with Jesus it may not always
have been successful.
But it inaugurated a new idea:
the idea of redemption,
the idea of giving a fresh object
of love and interest to the sinner,
and so freeing him from his sin.

C. G. Montefiore

Unless the grain of wheat
falls to the earth and dies,
it remains just a grain of wheat.
But if it dies,
it produces much fruit.
The man who loves his life loses it,
while the man who hates his life in this world
preserves it to life eternal.

John 12:24–25

"The man who wants to save his own life will lose it," he said, "But the man who loses his life for my sake will find it."

It might be printed in an Alpine guide
or a drill book.
This paradox is the whole principle of courage,
even of quite earthy or quite brutal courage.
A man cut off by the sea
may save his life if he will risk it
on the precipice.
He can get away from death
only by continually stepping
within an inch of it.
A soldier surrounded by enemies,
if he is to cut his way out,
needs to combine a strong desire for living
with a strange carelessness about dying.
He must not merely cling to life,
for then he will be a coward
and will not excape.
He must not merely wait for death,
for then he will be a suicide
and will not escape.
He must seek his life
in a spirit of furious indifference to it;
he must desire life like water
and yet drink death like wine.

G. K. Chesterton

Son though he was,
he learned obedience
from what he suffered;
and when perfected,
he became the source
of eternal salvation
for all who obey him.
                Hebrews 5:8–9

But this is the covenant which I will make
with the house of Israel
after those days, says the Lord.
I will place my law within them,
and write it upon their hearts;
I will be their God,
and they shall be my people.
No longer will they have need
to teach their friends and kinsmen
how to know the Lord.
All, from least to greatest,
shall know me, says the Lord,
for I will forgive their evildoing
and remember their sin no more.
                Jeremiah 31:33–34

The Way of the Lord

When Jesus was in Bethany reclining at table
in the house of Simon the leper,
a woman entered carrying an alabaster jar
of perfume made from expensive aromatic nard.
Breaking the jar, she began to pour
the perfume on his head.
Some were saying to themselves indignantly:
"What is the point
of the extravagant waste of perfume?
It could have been sold for over three hundred silver piece
and the money given to the poor."
They were infuriated at her.
But Jesus said: "Let her alone.
Why do you criticize her?
She has done me a kindness.
The poor you will always have with you
and you can be generous to them
whenever you wish,
but you will not always have me.
She has done what she could.
By perfuming my body
she is anticipating its preparation for burial."

Mark 14:3-

Mortification is always and by definition an act of nonviolence. The good sense of nonviolence and the good sense of mortification are the same. Both believe in the redemptive power of suffering love. Both intend to move oppressors, beginning with oneself, to see all victims, beginning with oneself, as persons worthy of respect. Both believe that crucifixion reveals resurrection, that death opens the way to life.

Nonviolence and mortification both spring from the conviction that human life is inexpressibly good and that evil, even in its contemporary forms, is able to be transformed by the human capacity to suffer for love. It is there that God still chooses to live among us.

James Carroll

They brought the colt to Jesus
and threw their cloaks across its back,
and he sat on it.
Many people spread their cloaks on the road,
while others spread reeds
which they had cut in the fields.
Those preceding him
as well as those who followed cried out:
"Hosannah!
Blessed be he who comes
in the name of the Lord!
Blessed be the reign
of our father David to come!
God save him from on high!"

Mark 11:7–10

Jesus had deliberately chosen
the way of suffering and death;
it was forced upon him
by his consciousness of what he was.
There was no place
for the solitary son of God
upon this earth,
nor for a living Messiah in the world.
Having chosen his ineluctable destiny,
he made his face rigid
to go to Jerusalem.
He had chosen to die in Jerusalem,
and to die at the feast of the Passover.
He would be the sacrificial lamb
of his people and the world:
"as the sheep before the shearers is dumb,
so he would open not his mouth."

J. Middleton Murry

Christ became obedient for us
even to death
dying on the cross.
Therefore God raised him on high
and gave him a name
above all other names.

Phillipians 2:8–9

The Table of the Lord

"This day shall be a memorial feast for you,
which all your generations
shall celebrate with pilgrimage
to the Lord,
as a perpetual institution."

Exodus 12:14

We need to break out of the bareness
of the exclusively rational and verbal
and find expression
through the use of ancient symbols
so that contemporary meanings
may be completed, purified, and transformed
by the meanings of the faith
as they meet in symbolic action.

Reuel L. Howe

Simon Peter said to him,
"Lord, are you going to wash my feet?"
Jesus answered, "You may not realize now
what I am doing, but later you will understand."
Peter replied, "You shall never wash my feet!"
"If I do not wash you," Jesus answered,
"you will have no share in my heritage."
"Lord," Simon Peter said to him,
"then not only my feet,
but my hands and head as well."

John 13:6–9

I received from the Lord
what I handed on to you,
namely, that the Lord Jesus
on the night in which he was betrayed
took bread, and after he had given thanks,
broke it and said,
"This is my body, which is for you.
Do this in remembrance of me."

1 Corinthians 11:23–24

Symbols have the avowed purpose
of opening up dimensions of reality and truth
which would otherwise remain hidden
and cannot be grasped in any other way.
They are truly adequate,
even rationally adequate, to the extent
to which they point beyond themselves
and so communicate their own inadequacy.
Perhaps it is paradoxical to say so,
but the more transparent a symbol is
to the transcendence that inspires it,
the truer and more meaningful it is.

Roger Hazelton

To experience the mystery of Christ . . .
is always to transcend
the merely individual psychological level
and to "experience theologically with the Church."
In other words, this experience must always be
in some way reducible to a theological form
that can be shared by the rest of the Church
or that shows that it is a sharing
of what the rest of the Church experiences.
There is therefore in the recording
of Christian experiences
a natural tendency to set them down
in language and symbols
that are easily accessible to other Christians.
This may perhaps sometimes mean
an unconscious translation of the inexpressible
into familiar symbols
that are always at hand
ready for immediate use.

Thomas Merton

The Suffering Servant

Because of his affliction
he shall see the light in fullness of days;
Through his suffering,
my servant shall justify many,
and their guilt he shall bear.
Therefore I will give him
his portion among the great,
and he shall divide the spoils with the mighty,
Because he surrendered himself to death
and was counted among the wicked;
And he shall take away the sins of many,
and win pardon for their offenses.

Isaiah 53:11–12

Judas took the cohort as well as guards
supplied by the chief priests and the Pharisees,
and came there with lanterns, torches and weapons.
Jesus, aware of all that would happen to him,
stepped forward and said to them,
"Who is it you want?"
"Jesus the Nazorean," they replied.
"I am he," he answered.
(Now Judas, the one who was to hand him over,
was right there with them.)
As Jesus said to them, "I am he,"
they retreated slightly and fell to the ground.
Jesus put the question to them again,
"Who is it you want?"
"Jesus the Nazorean," they repeated.
"I have told you, I am he," Jesus said.

John 18:3–8

O Savior Christ, Thou too art Man;
Thou has been troubled, tempted, tried;
Thy kind but searching glance can scan
The very wounds that shame would hide.
                                    Henry Twells

Until the last day he remained for the people
the prophet from Nazareth.
It is the latter, not the Messiah,
who receives the ovation
at the entry into Jerusalem.
Even the Pharisees and the Scribes,
who come to terms with him during the last days,
have no suspicion of his claims;
otherwise they would have brought it up for discussion.
One is aware that the High Priest
is not able to summon a single witness at the trial
to testify to the Messianic claims of Jesus.

Albert Schweitzer

We have a great high priest
who has passed through the heavens,
Jesus, the Son of God;
let us hold fast to our profession of faith.
For we do not have a high priest
who is unable to sympathize
with our weakness,
but one who was tempted
in every way that we are,
yet never sinned.
So let us confidently approach
the throne of grace
to receive mercy and favor
and to find help in time of need.

Hebrews 4:14–16

Risen with Christ

What do we mean by "God"?
Not in the first place an abstract belief
in his omnipotence, etc.
That is not a genuine experience of God,
but a partial extension of the world.
Encounter with Jesus Christ,
implying a complete orientation
of human being
in the experience of Jesus
as one whose only concern
is for others.
This concern of Jesus for others,
the experience of transcendence . . .
Our relation to God
not a religious relationship
to a supreme Being,
absolute in power and goodness,
which is a spurious conception
of transcendence,
but a new life for others,
through participation
in the Being of God.
The transcendence consists
not in tasks beyond our scope and power,
but in the nearest thou to hand.
God in human form . . .
man existing for others,
and hence the Crucified.
A life based on the transcendent.

Dietrich Bonhoeffer

On entering the tomb
they saw a young man sitting at the right,
dressed in a white robe.
This frightened them thoroughly,
but he reassured them:
"You need not be amazed!
You are looking for Jesus of Nazareth,
the one who was crucified.
He has been raised up;
he is not here.
See the place where they laid him.
Go now and tell his disciples and Peter,
'He is going ahead of you to Galilee,
where you will see him
just as he told you!' "

Mark 16:5–7

For a brief moment I abandoned you,
but with great tenderness I will take you back.
In an outburst of wrath, for a moment
I hid my face from you;
But with enduring love I take pity on you,
says the Lord, your redeemer . . .
Though the mountains leave their place
and the hills be shaken,
My love shall never leave you
nor my covenant of peace be shaken,
says the Lord, who has mercy on you.

                    Isaiah 54:7–8, 10

Are you not aware that we
who were baptized into Christ Jesus
were baptized into his death?
Through baptism into his death
we were buried with him,
so that, just as Christ
was raised from the dead
by the glory of the Father,
we too might live a new life.
If we have been united with him
through likeness to his death,
so shall we be
through a like resurrection.

                    Romans 6:3–5

About a quarter before nine,
while he was describing the change
which God works in the heart
through faith in Christ,
I felt my heart strangely warmed.
I felt I did trust in Christ,
Christ alone for salvation;
and an assurance was given me
that he had taken away my sins,
even mine, and saved me
from the law of sin and death.

I began to pray with all my might
for those who had
in a more especial manner
despitefully used me
and persecuted me.

                    John Wesley

THE
DAYS
OF
EASTER

Easter: Resurrection and Life

Peter and the other disciple
started out on their way toward the tomb.
They were running side by side,
but then the other disciple outran Peter
and reached the tomb first.
He did not enter but bent down to peer in,
and saw the wrappings lying on the ground.
Presently, Simon Peter came along behind him
and entered the tomb . . .
Then the disciple who had arrived first
at the tomb went in.
He saw and believed.

John 20:3–6, 8

Do you not know that a little yeast
has its effect all through the dough?
Get rid of the old yeast
to make of yourselves fresh dough,
unleavened loaves, as it were;
Christ our Passover has been sacrificed.
Let us celebrate the feast
not with the old yeast,
that of corruption and wickedness,
but with the unleavened bread
of sincerity and truth.

1 Corinthians 5:6–8

I knew that I was done with sin;
I knew that Christ had given me birth
To brother all the souls on earth.
                              John Masefield

"He commissioned us
to preach to the people
and to bear witness
that he is the one
set apart by God
as judge of the living and the dead.
To him all the prophets testify,
saying that everyone who believes in him
has forgiveness of sins
through his name."

Acts 10:42–43

I am the Resurrection and the Life.

If any other human lips could ever have made
a measurable fraction of such a claim
it would have sounded like an insane boast.
It is only because the claim
is not fractional, but complete,
that it has never occurred to any one
to regard it as a "boast"
or as incompatible with a divine humility.
The utterance is its own evidence,
as no other ever has been;
for its kingdom, its infinitude, is within it.
Any madman might say things
equally impossible from the human point of view;
but he could not simultaneously
overwhelm us with that strange sense
of the infinitely holy,
or move the depths of innumerable hearts
to adoration for two thousand years
by the sheer majesty—
and awful humility—of his words.
We might also say
that the supreme claim of the words
would be utterly intolerable
if they were not true.
But the words have been cherished
in the hearts of countless millions,
to whom they conveyed the values of God . . .

Alfred Noyes

The Community of Believers

I believe that we are discovering again
these old facts:
The only reason to be the church
is to be religious;
the only reason to be religious
is to pray;
the only reason to pray
is to love God;
the only reason to love God
is to love the world;
the only reason to love the world
is to love each other.

                                    James Carroll

Everyone who believes
that Jesus is the Christ
has been begotten by God . . .
Everyone begotten of God
conquers the world,
and the power
that has conquered the world
is this faith of ours.
Who, then, is conqueror of the world?
The one who believes
that Jesus is the Son of God.

                             1 John 5:1, 4–5

The community of believers
were of one heart and one mind.
None of them ever claimed
anything as his own;
rather everything was held in common.
With power the apostles bore witness
to the resurrection of the Lord Jesus,
and great respect was paid to them all.

Acts 4:32–33

I was astonished to discover
that no mere intellectual acceptance
of Christ's divinity
would have satisfied Jesus
as a way of entrance into his kingdom.
He will settle for nothing less
than making him
the ruler of one's life,
with the inevitable result
of a practical day-by-day obedience:
"Why do you call me Lord, Lord,
and not do the things which I say?"
No wonder marching down
the church aisle
had not changed me one whit.

Catherine Marshall

The disciples were once more in the room,
and this time Thomas was with them.
Despite the locked doors,
Jesus came and stood before them.
"Peace be with you," he said;
then, to Thomas: "Take your finger
and examine my hands.
Put your hand into my side.
Do not persist in your unbelief,
but believe!"
Thomas said in response,
"My Lord and my God!"
Jesus then said to him:
"You became a believer because you saw me.
Blest are they who have not seen
and have believed."

John 20:26–29

His Witnesses

While they were still speaking about all this,
he himself stood in their midst
and said to them, "Peace to you." . . .
Then he said to them,
"Recall those words I spoke to you
when I was still with you:
everything written about me
in the law of Moses
and the prophets and psalms
had to be fulfilled."
Then he opened their minds
to the understanding of the Scriptures.
He said to them: "Thus it is likewise written
that the Messiah must suffer
and rise from the dead on the third day.
In his name, penance for the remission of sins
is to be preached to all the nations,
beginning at Jerusalem.
You are witnesses of this."

Luke 24:36, 44–48

The story told in the Gospels
has been retold in every age
subsequent to the time of Christ.
It has been told differently, though,
according to the different
preoccupations of each epoch.
In our time it is told characteristically, it seems,
as an "answer to Job,"
as a solution to the problem of human suffering.
As it is told, for example, by Camus in *The Rebel*
or by Jung in the *Answer to Job*,
it begins with the problem
posed in the Book of Job
and goes from there to the solution
found in the Gospels.
The problem is that man suffers,
and his suffering cannot be explained away
by saying that he has sinned
and brought it all upon himself.
The solution then is that God,
instead of taking away the suffering,
himself becomes man
and shares the suffering.

John S. Dunne

Jesus Christ . . . is an offering for our sins,
and not for our sins only,
but for those of the whole world.

1 John 2:2

"You put to death the Author of life.
But God raised him from the dead,
and we are his witnesses.
Yet I know, my brothers,
that you acted out of ignorance,
just as your leaders did.
God has brought to fulfillment by this means
what he announced long ago
through all the prophets:
that his Messiah would suffer.
Therefore, reform your lives!
Turn to God,
that your sins may be wiped away!"
                                        Acts 3:15–19

We must continue to stress
that Christ is indeed
the center of human existence,
the center of history
and now, too, the center of nature;
but these three aspects
can be distinguished only in the abstract.
In fact, human existence
is always history, always nature as well.
As fulfiller of the law
and liberator of creation,
the mediator acts
for the whole of human existence.
He is the same,
who is intercessor and *pro me*,
and who is himself
the end of the old world
and the beginning of the new world of God.
                            Dietrich Bonhoeffer

Jesus Our Savior

"I know my sheep
and my sheep know me
in the same way
that the Father knows me
and I know the Father;
for these sheep I will give my life.
I have other sheep
that do not belong to this fold.
I must lead them, too,
and they shall hear my voice.
There shall be one flock then,
one shepherd."

John 10:14–16

The Gospel, however, is not merely
about a free man;
it is the good news of a free man
who has set other men free,
first proclaimed by those
to whom this had happened . . .
Their response, which the New Testament
calls "faith,"
consists in acknowledging
that this has happened
by accepting the liberator,
Jesus of Nazareth,
as the man who defines for them
what it means to be a man
and as the point of orientation
for their lives.

Paul van Buren

We are God's children now;
what we shall later be
has not yet come to light.
We know that when it comes to light
we shall be like him,
for we shall see him as he is.

1 John 3:2

Seeing him alone,
one transcends death;
there is no other way.
      Svetasvatara Upanishad

The earliest Christianity of the first disciples
was devotion to a person—
"Follow me," he said.
It was not a formal creed nor an ethical code
but a Man they believed in.
He was to them that most powerful force
in human experience,
an incarnation, embodying and revealing
in his own person
the truths he represented.
When they thought of God,
it was more and more in terms of Jesus:
when they thought of goodness,
it meant likeness to him.
So he became to them not only Teacher,
but Lord and Savior,
revealer of the divine,
ideal of the human,
who having died for their sakes
still lived,
and to whom, in God's good time,
the future belonged.

                    Harry Emerson Fosdick

"This Jesus is the 'stone rejected
by you the builders
which has become the cornerstone.'
There is no salvation in anyone else,
for there is no other name
in the whole world given to men
by which we are to be saved."

                    Acts 4:11–12

Live on in Me

To think about Jesus today
is to become aware that we are responsible
for the most dynamic civilization
the world has ever seen.
In this secular vineyard we are confronted
by the coming of this man, Jesus of Nazareth,
who reminds us of our true situation.
He comes with God's demands
that he receive his due, that requirement—
to "do justly, to love mercy
and to walk humbly with your God" (Micah 6:8)—
with which mankind is confronted.
As with the men in the old story,
so with us.
Whether we listen to this man Jesus
or crucify him afresh,
the words "when the owner of the vineyard comes"
signify our future, as they did theirs.

Geoffrey Ainger

"Live on in me, as I do in you.
No more than a branch
can bear fruit of itself
apart from the vine,
can you bear fruit
apart from me.
I am the vine, you are the branches.
He who lives in me and I in him,
will produce abundantly."

John 15:4–5

Let us love in deed and in truth
and not merely talk about it.
This is our way of knowing
we are committed to the truth
and are at peace before him
no matter what our consciences
may charge us with;
for God is greater than our hearts
and all is known to him.

1 John 3:18–20

Lord, make me an instrument of thy
    peace.
Where there is hate, may I bring
    love;
Where offense, may I bring pardon;
May I bring union in place of discord;
Truth, replacing error;
Faith, where once there was doubt;
Hope, for despair;
Light, where was darkness;
Joy to replace sadness.
Make me not to so crave to be loved
    as to love.
Help me to learn that in giving I may
    receive;
In forgetting self, I may find life
    eternal.

               St. Francis of Assisi

Throughout all Judea, Galilee and Samaria
the church was at peace.
It was being built up
and was making steady progress
in the fear of the Lord;
at the same time it enjoyed
the increased consolation
of the Holy Spirit.

Acts 9:31

Lady: This needs to be explained. If you are right, why is it that Christ is called the Prince of Peace, and why did he say that peacemakers will be called the children of God?

Mr. Z: And you are so kind that you wish me also to obtain that higher distinction by making peace between contradictory texts?

Lady: I do wish it.

Mr. Z: Then, please note that the only way of making peace between them is by distinguishing between the good or true peace and the bad or wrong peace. This distinction was clearly pointed out by him who brought us the true peace and the good enmity: "My peace I leave with you, My peace I give unto you. Not as the world giveth, give I unto you." There is therefore the good peace—the peace of Christ resting on the *division* which Christ came to bring to the world, namely, the division between good and evil, between truth and untruth. There is also bad peace—the peace of the world which endeavors to blend or to unite together externally elements which internally are at war with one another.

Vladimir Soloviev

109

The God Who Is Love

Jesus Christ alone
founded his empire
upon love,
and at this hour
millions of men would die for him . . .
The religion of Christ
is a mystery which subsists
by its own force,
and proceeds from a mind
which is not a human mind.
Jesus exhibited in himself
the perfect example
of his precepts.
Jesus came into the world to reveal
the mysteries of heaven
and the laws of the Spirit.

Napoleon Bonaparte

Let us love one another
because love is God;
everyone who loves is begotten of God
and has knowledge of God.
The man without love
has known nothing of God,
for God is love . . .
Love, then, consists in this:
not that we have loved God,
but that he has loved us
and has sent his Son
as an offering for our sins.

1 John 4:7–8, 10

"As the Father has loved me,
so I have loved you.
Live on in my love.
You will live in my love
if you keep my commandments,
even as I have kept
my Father's commandments,
and live in his love.
All this I tell you
that my joy may be yours
and your joy may be complete.
This is my commandment:
love one another
as I have loved you.
There is no greater love than this:
to lay down one's life for one's friends."

John 15:9–13

Peter proceeded to address
the relatives and friends of Cornelius
in these words: "I begin to see
how true it is that God shows no partiality.
Rather, the man of any nation
who fears God and acts uprightly
is acceptable to him."
Peter had not finished these words
when the Holy Spirit descended
upon all who were listening
to Peter's message.
The circumcised believers
who had accompanied Peter
were suprised that the gift
of the Holy Spirit
should have been poured out
on the Gentiles also
whom they could hear speaking in tongues
and glorifying God.
Peter put the question at that point:
"What can stop these people
who have received the Holy Spirit,
even as we have,
from being baptized with water?"
So he gave orders that they be baptized
in the name of Jesus Christ.

                    Acts 10:34–35, 44–48

The fundamental virtue
in the ethics of Jesus
was love,
because love is the society-making quality.
Human life originates in love.
It is love that holds together
the basal human organization, the family.
The physical expression
of all love and friendship
is the desire to get together
and be together.
Love creates fellowship.
In the measure in which love
increases in any social organism,
it will hold together without coercion.
If physical coercion is constantly necessary,
it is proof that the social organization
has not evoked the power
of human affection and fraternity.

Hence when Jesus prepared men
for the nobler social order of the kingdom of God,
he tried to energize
the faculty and habits of love
and to stimulate the dormant faculty
of devotion to the common good.

Walter Rauschenbusch

The Master and His Disciples

Jesus, appearing to the Eleven, said to them:
"Go into the whole world
and proclaim the good news
to all creation.
The man who believes in it
and accepts baptism will be saved;
the man who refuses to believe in it
will be condemned.
Signs like these will accompany
those who have professed their faith:
they will use my name to expel demons,
they will speak entirely new languages,
they will be able to handle serpents,
they will be able to drink
deadly poison without harm,
and the sick upon whom
they lay their hands will recover."

Mark 16:15–18

In my first account, Theophilus,
I dealt with all that Jesus did and taught
until the day he was taken up to heaven,
having first instructed the apostles
he had chosen through the Holy Spirit.
In the time after his suffering
he showed them in many convincing ways
that he was alive,
appearing to them
over the course of forty days
and speaking to them
about the reign of God.

Acts 1:1–3

Whenever our civilization wants
a library to be cataloged,
or a solar system discovered,
or any trifles of that kind,
it uses its specialists.
But when it wishes anything done
which is really serious,
is collects twelve of the ordinary men
standing around.
The same thing was done,
if I remember right,
by the Founder of Christianity.

G. K. Chesterton

He comes to us
as One unknown,
without a name,
as of old, by the lakeside,
he came to those men
who knew him not.
He speaks to us the same word:
"Follow thou me!"
and sets us the tasks
which he has to fulfil for our time.
He commands.
And to those who obey him,
whether they be wise or simple,
he will reveal himself
in the toils,
the conflicts,
the sufferings
which they shall pass through
in his fellowship,
and as an ineffable mystery,
they shall learn in their own experience
who he is.

Albert Schweitzer

The strangeness of Jesus
is not his common humanity with us.
His common humanity
we have established for our century
and take for granted—
at least the people outside the churches do!
The strangeness is something other.

The strangeness is in what he was
that caused others to call him
"Rabbi," "Master," "Lord,"
and even, afterwards, "God."
The strangeness is in the arbitrariness,
the oddness of this tiny incident
in a backwater of the Roman Empire,
which the historians hardly mention—
that of becoming the faith and the life
which overcame empires,
which overcame religions,
which overcame death.
And it was not any *deus ex machina*
that did it. It was *he*!

John J. Vincent

May the God of our Lord Jesus Christ,
the Father of glory,
grant you a spirit of wisdom and insight
to know him clearly.
May he enlighten your innermost vision
that you may know the great hope
to which he has called you,
the wealth of his glorious heritage
to be distributed among the members of the church,
and the immeasurable scope of his power
in us who believe.

Esphesians 1:17–19

A Teaching Church

"I say all this while I am still in the world
that they may share my joy completely.
I gave them your word,
and the world has hated them for it;
they do not belong to the world,
any more than I belong to the world . . .
As you have sent me into the world,
so I have sent them into the world;
I consecrate myself for their sakes now,
that they may be consecrated in truth."

John 17:13–14, 19–20

All through his life, Christ felt the privations and tasted the joys of poverty. On his own testimony, he was hungry, thirsty, and without a place whereon to lay his head. Nor was this a condemnation of riches. It was no secret in Christ's time that riches can be an occasion of pride and offer opportunites for sins that are not open to the poor man; but then neither were the men of that time ignorant of the fact that poverty can be no less an occasion of sin, indeed, an occasion of all those sins a man will commit to seize the riches upon which his heart is set. It is neither riches nor poverty that count; but the poverty of spirit which is a casting aside of the trinkets of the world in the realization of how little they contribute to the perfection of man's life.

Walter Farrell

118

We have seen for ourselves, and can testify,
that the Father has sent the Son
as savior of the world.
When anyone acknowledges
that Jesus is the Son of God,
God dwells in him
and he in God.
We have come to know and to believe
in the love God has for us.

1 John 4:14–16

The Church has a stake
in the totality of human knowledge,
for it is in terms of this totality
that she must explain her message to the world,
and, indeed, that her members
must hold her message in their own consciousness.
Because of the relationship of revelation
to natural knowledge,
and to growing natural knowledge,
it seems quite accurate to state
that one reason why the Church is devoted
to higher education in the secular subjects
is to educate herself
in what is absolutely essential for her mission.

Walter J. Ong

"It is entirely fitting, therefore,
that one of those
who was of our company
while the Lord Jesus moved among us,
from the baptism of John until the day
he was taken up from us,
should be named as witness with us
to his resurrection."
At that they nominated two,
Joseph (called Barsabbas, also known as Justus)
and Matthias.
Then they prayed: "O Lord,
you read the hearts of men.
Make known to us which of these two
you choose for this apostolic ministry,
replacing Judas, who deserted the cause
and went the way he was destined to go."
They then drew lots
between the two men.
The choice fell to Matthias,
who was added to the eleven apostles.

Acts 1:21–26

The concept of Christian service
as a function of the Church
should place the Church in the vanguard
of those who wish to improve education,
implement better welfare programs,
care for the poverty-plagued millions
in the world today
and stimulate the progress
of scientific and technological programs
that will assist the human community
to enjoy more truly human lives.

Leon McKenzie

THE
COMING
OF
THE
HOLY
SPIRIT

The Coming of the Spirit

On the evening of that first day of the week,
even though the disciples had locked the doors
of the place where they were
for fear of the Jews,
Jesus came and stood before them.
"Peace be with you," he said.
When he had said this,
he showed them his hands and his side.
At the sight of the Lord
the disciples rejoiced.
"Peace be with you," he said again . . .
The he breathed on them and said:
"Receive the Holy Spirit."

John 20:19–21

The body is one and has many members,
but all the members,
many though they are,
are one body;
and so it is with Christ.
It was in one Spirit that all of us,
whether Jew or Greek, slave or free,
were baptized into one body.
All of us have been given
to drink of the one Spirit.

1 Corinthians 12:12–13

Staying in Jerusalem at the time
were devout Jews
of every nation under heaven.
These heard the sound,
and assembled in a large crowd.
They were much confused
because each one heard these men
speaking his own language.
The whole occurrence astonished them.
They asked in utter amazement,
"Are not all of these men
who are speaking Galileans? . . .
Yet each of us hears them speaking
in his own tongue
about the marvels God has accomplished."

Acts 2:5–7, 11

I speak of the faith
which in acting upon a life
transforms it,
the faith which tries
to be worthy of forgiveness
before even asking
for deliverance and help,
the faith which illumines,
and strengthens,
and softens souls
by communion with divine life;
the faith which leads
to that life in God, and for God,
which lifts up and magnifies all life.
I speak of the Holy Spirit
which would renew
the face of the earth,
if the world would open wide
to take him in.

France Pastorelli

The new world was not just
something that *would* come
if only people followed the teaching.
It was something that *was coming*
whether they followed it or not.
It was "the Kingdom" . . .

It would be a total
misunderstanding of the matter
to say that Jesus merely used
the idea of a kingdom
to get across his 'purely spiritual' message,
accepting the political overtones
as an occupational hazard.
As though there was merely the risk
that the more hasty among his hearers
would twist his words to a political meaning . . .

It is truer to say that his words
had *no other* meaning than the political,
no other meaning within the human range,
and that their further meaning
could only be created
by the outpouring Spirit . . .

His whole ethic of non-resistance to evil,
which in privileged moments of light
reveals itself as practical politics,
was put into practice by Jesus
at the centre of the human vortex.
And there the human,
reduced to its ultimate logic
in a violent death,
was filled with the Spirit
and issued in the resurrection.

Sebastian Moore

Father, Son, Spirit

The matter of greatest moment
is to observe the Spirit of God
revealing itself in history,
enlightening and directing the judgments of men,
saving and guiding mankind,
and, even here below, admonishing,
judging and chastising nations and generations.
This threefold law of the world,
these three mighty principles
which dominate the historical development of mankind—
the hidden ways of a Providence
which delivers and emancipates the human race;
the free-will of man,
compelled to make a decisive choice
in the struggle of life,
in all of its acts
and in the feelings to which it gives rise;
and the power given by God to the evil principle—
cannot be posited as absolutely necessary,
as are the phenomena of nature
or the laws of human reason.
It is, rather, in the characteristic marks
of particular events and historical facts
that the visible traces
of invisible power and design,
of high and hidden wisdom,
must be sought for.

Friedrich Schlegel

128

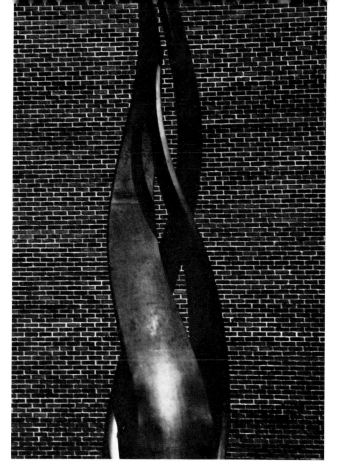

"Full authority has been given to me
both in heaven and on earth;
go, therefore, and make disciples
of all the nations.
Baptize them in the name
'of the Father
and of the Son,
and of the Holy Spirit.'
Teach them to carry out
everything I have commanded you.
And know that I am with you always,
until the end of the world!"

Matthew 28:18–20

All who are led by the Spirit of God
are sons of God . . .
The Spirit himself gives witness with our spirit
that we are children of God.
But if we are children,
we are heirs as well: heirs of God,
heirs with Christ,
if only we suffer with him
so as to be glorified with him.

Romans 8:14, 16–17

"You must now know,
and fix in your heart,
that the Lord is God
in the heavens above
and on earth below,
and that there is no other.
You must keep his statutes
and commandments
which I enjoin on you today,
that you and your children after you
may prosper,
and that you may have long life
on the land which the Lord, your God,
is giving you forever."

Deuteronomy 4:39-40

God is not far away from us,
altogether apart from the world we see,
touch, hear, smell and taste about us.
Rather he awaits us every instant
in our action, in the work of the moment.
There is a sense in which he is
at the tip of my pen, my spade, my brush, my needle—
of my heart and of my thought.
By pressing the stroke, the line, or the stitch,
on which I am engaged,
to its ultimate natural finish,
I shall lay hold of the last end
towards which my innermost will tends.

Pierre Teilhard de Chardin

The Call of God

John was in Bethany across the Jordan
with two of his disciples.
As he watched Jesus walk by he said,
"Look! There is the lamb of God!"
The two disciples heard what he said,
and followed Jesus.
When Jesus turned around
and noticed them following him,
he asked them, "What are you looking for?"
They said to him, "Rabbi
(which means Teacher),
where do you stay?"
"Come and see," he answered.
So they went to see where he was lodged,
and stayed with him that day.
(It was about four in the afternoon.)

John 1:35–39

Whoever is joined to the Lord
becomes one spirit with him . . .
You must know that your body
is a temple of the Holy Spirit,
who is within—
the Spirit you have received from God.
You are not your own.
You have been purchased,
and at what a price!
So glorify God in your body.

1 Corinthians 6:17, 19–20

The Lord called Samuel again, for the third time. Getting up and going to Eli, he said, "Here I am. You called me."

Then Eli understood that the Lord was calling the youth. So he said to Samuel, "Go to sleep, and if you are called, reply, 'Speak, Lord, for your servant is listening.' "

When Samuel went to sleep in his place, the Lord came and revealed his presence, calling out as before, "Samuel, Samuel!" Samuel answered, "Speak, for your servant is listening."

Samuel grew up, and the Lord was with him, not permitting any word of his to be without effect.

1 Samuel 3:8–10, 19

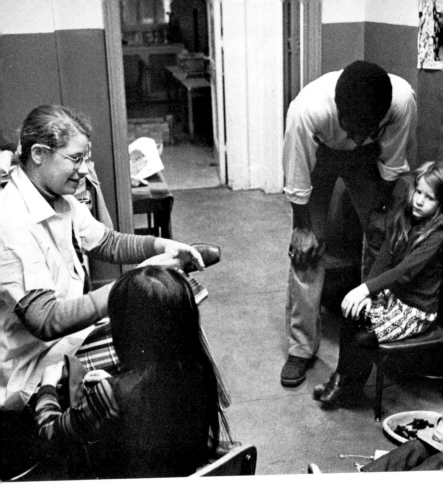

The description of God as a Person
is indispensable for everyone
who like myself means by "God"
not a principle . . .
not an idea . . .
but who rather means by "God," as I do,
him who—whatever else he may be—
enters into a direct relation with us men
in creative, revealing and redeeming acts,
and thus makes it possible for us

to enter into a direct relation with him.
This ground and meaning of our existence
constitutes a mutuality,
arising again and again,
such as can subsist only between persons.
The concept of personal being
is ineed completely incapable
of declaring what God's essential being is,
but it is both permitted and necessary
to say God is *also* a Person . . .

Martin Buber

Those who have been mentally blinded
"in the gradual furnace of the world"
can, and must, be pressed to look
for new capabilities within themselves
and work out new ways to happiness.
They may even resent faith
that expects nobler things from them.
They say in effect, "I will be content
if you take me for what I am—
dull, or mean, or hard, or selfish."
But it is an affront to them
and to the eternal dignity of man
so to acquiesce.
How often it comes over us that
there is much in us
which our nearest friends cannot know—
more than we dare or care
or are able to lay bare,
more of feeling,
more of power,
more of manhood.
How little we know ourselves!

Helen Keller

Reforming Our Lives

Mortification is not
the cultivation of private pain.
It is not an act of mere piety.
Whether it involves old-fashioned practices
like "giving up" candy
or more faddish experiments with organic food,
it is an instinct of discipline and control
which accepts limits as positive and creative.
And today, in a unique way,
mortification implies a political decision
against the politics of hedonism
and against the economics of consumerism.

James Carroll

Jonah began his journey through the city,
and had gone but a single day's walk
announcing, "Forty days more
and Nineveh shall be destroyed,"
when the people of Nineveh believed God;
they proclaimed a fast and all of them,
great and small, put on sackcloth.
When God saw by their actions
how they turned from their evil way,
he repented of the evil
that he had threatened to do to them;
he did not carry it out.

Jonah 3:4–5, 10

I tell you, brothers, the time is short.
From now on those with wives
should live as though they had none;
those who weep should live
as though they were not weeping,
and those who rejoice
as though they were not rejoicing;
buyers should conduct themselves
as though they owned nothing,
and those who make use of the world
as though they were not using it,
for the world as we know it is passing away.

1 Corinthians 7:29–31

After John's arrest,
Jesus appeared in Galilee
proclaiming God's good news:
"This is the time of fulfillment.
The reign of God is at hand!
Reform your lives and believe
in the good news!"

Mark 1:14–15

To have faith requires *courage*,
the ability to take a risk,
the readiness even to accept pain
and disappointment.
Whoever insists on safety and security
as primary conditions of life
cannot have faith;
whoever shuts himself off in a system of defense,
where distance and possession
are his means of security,
makes himself a prisoner.
To be loved, and to love,
need courage, the courage to judge certain values
as of ultimate concern—
and to take the jump
and stake everything on these values.

Erich Fromm

Pleasures *can* be provided
and pain *can* be avoided,
if we use or abuse other beings.
But joy cannot be attained
and sorrow cannot be overcome in this way.
Joy is possible only when we are driven
towards things and persons
because of what they are
and not because of what we can get from them.

Paul Tillich

A New Teaching

I have no desire
to place restrictions on you,
but I do want to promote
what is good,
what will help you
to devote yourselves
entirely to the Lord.

               1 Corinthians 7:35

"I will raise up for them a prophet like you
from among their kinsmen,
and will put my words into his mouth;
he shall tell them all
that I command him.
If any man will not listen to my words
which he speaks in my name,
I myself will make him answer for it."
                                    Deuteronomy 18:18–19

There appeared in their synagogue
a man with an unclean spirit that shrieked:
"What do you want of us, Jesus of Nazareth?
Have you come to destroy us?
I know who you are—
the holy One of God!"
Jesus rebuked him sharply:
"Be quiet! Come out of the man!"
At that the unclean spirit convulsed the man violently
and with a loud shriek came out of him.
All who looked on were amazed.
They began to ask one another:
"What does this mean?
A completely new teaching in a spirit of authority!
He gives orders to unclean spirits
and they obey him!"
From that point on his reputation spread
throughout the surrounding region of Galilee.
                                            Mark 1:23–28

In the most remote times, long before the day
of any of these pretended philosophers,
there lived certain men,
happy, just and beloved by God,
who spoke by the Holy Spirit
and foretold many things
that have since come to pass.
We call them prophets . . .
Their writings still remain
and those who read them with faith
draw much and various profit,
concerning both the beginning and the end,
and all a philosopher ought to know.
They did not deal in demonstrations;
for far above all demonstration
they were worthy witnesses to the truth.

                                            St. Justin

It is impossible to deny to the true believer,
who experiences in himself
what he calls the effects of grace,
who finds his repose
and all the peace of his soul
in the intervention
of certain ideas or intellectual acts
of faith, hope and charity,
and who thus succeeds in satisfying his mind
on problems which all the systems have left unsolved,
it is impossible, I say,
to contest his experience,
and to fail to recognize how well founded
either in himself or in his religious beliefs,
are those states of soul
which make his consolation and his happiness.

                                          Maine de Biran

The Demands of Service

At the root of Christian service must be
the virtue, the power, of Christian love.
Christian service is precisely Christian
because it is motivated
neither by the avarice of heartless capitalism
nor by an overriding concern for the faceless state,
but by love of the individual who is served.

Leon McKenzie

I have been assigned months of misery,
and troubled nights have been told off for me.
If in bed I say, "When shall I arise?"
then the night drags on;
I am filled with restlessness until the dawn.

Job 7:3–4

Preaching the gospel is not the subject of a boast;
I am under compulsion and have no choice.
I am ruined if I do not preach it!
If I do it willingly, I have my recompense;
if unwillingly, I am nonetheless entrusted with a charge.
And this recompense of mine?
It is simply this, that when preaching
I offer the gospel free of charge . . .
I do all that I do for the sake of the gospel
in the hope of having a share in its blessings.

1 Corinthians 9:16–18, 23

144

To be a man
is to suffer for others.
God help us to be men.
                Caesar Chavez

Rising early the next morning,
he went off to a lonely place in the desert;
there he was absorbed in prayer.
Simon and his companions
managed to track him down;
and when they found him, they told him,
"Everybody is looking for you!"
He said to them: "Let us move on
to the neighboring villages
so that I may proclaim
the good news there also.
That is what I have come to do."
So he went into their synagogues
preaching the good news . . .

Mark 1:35–39

Only an absolutely sound body
could have been equal to such demands on it.
Moreover, this wandering life
was filled to overflowing
with labor and toil.
Again and again Mark notes the fact
that they had not time to eat.
Till late in the evening
the sick kept coming and going.
And with the sick there came malevolent enemies,
the Pharisees and Sadducees,
and word wrestled with word,
mind with mind,
and racking disputes took place,
leading to dangerous moments of tension and conflict.
In additon there were the tiring explanations
he had to make to his own disciples
and the heavy burden which
their want of understanding
and their self-seeking laid upon him.
Any sickly or even weak constitution
must have given in or broken down
under the strain.
That Jesus never on any occasion gave in,
not even in the most tense or dangerous situations,
that, for instance, in the midst
of a raging storm on the Lake of Genesareth
he went on peacefully sleeping
until his disciples woke him,
and that suddenly roused from his deep sleep
he immediately grasped the situation
and dealt with it,
all this is proof how far his nature was
from being excitable and temperamental,
what complete control he had over his senses,
how sound he was in body.

Karl Adam

Christ the Healer

Jesus' chief motive in healing
seems rather to have been
nothing more or less
than pure compassion.
The word *compassion*
is used over and over
to describe his attitude
toward the sick.
That was why he often went
out of his way to heal
when the sufferer had neither
asked for nor thought of
his doing so.
He delighted in straightening
a bent back.
He rejoiced in that moment
when a man gleefully flings away
his crutches.
He was glad
that he could break up a funeral
and give a beloved son
back to his mother.
It was a gratifying thing to him
to see the light of reason and sanity
return to the eyes
of a violent demoniac.
Jesus healed because the love of God
flowing irresistibly through him
in a torrent of good will
simply swept evil away
as the debris that it is.

Catherine Marshall

"The one who bears the sore of leprosy
shall keep his garments rent and his head bare,
and shall muffle his beard;
he shall cry out, 'Unclean, unclean!'
As long as the sore is on him
he shall declare himself unclean
since he is in fact unclean.
He shall dwell apart,
making his abode outside the camp."

                              Leviticus 13:45–46

The world that the Christian detests
consists of all that mass
of disorder, deformity and evil
introduced into creation
by man's own voluntary defection.
He turns away from these, no doubt,
but precisely to adhere with all his heart
to the order, beauty and good
which was willed from the beginning;
he works to restore these
in himself and others;
with an heroic effort
he would clear the face of the universe
and render it resplendent once more
as the face of God.
Nothing could be more positive
than such an asceticism,
nothing could be better grounded in hope . . .

                              Étienne Gilson

A leper approached Jesus with a request,
kneeling down as he addressed him:
"If you will to do so, you can cure me."
Moved with pity, Jesus stretched out his hand,
touched him, and said:
"I do will it. Be cured."
The leprosy left him then and there,
and he was cured.
Jesus gave him a stern warning
and sent him on his way.
"Not a word to anyone, now." he said.
"Go off and present yourself to the priest
and offer for your cure what Moses prescribed.
That should be a proof for them."
The man went off and began
to proclaim the whole matter freely,
making the story public.
As a result of this, it was no longer possible
for Jesus to enter a town openly.
He stayed in desert places;
yet people kept coming to him from all sides.

Mark 1:40–45

Give no offense to Jew or Greek
or to the church of God,
just as I try to please all
in any way I can
by seeking not my own advantage,
but that of the many
that they may be saved.

1 Corinthians 10:32–33

Your Sins Are Forgiven

And so you can't change yourself with books.
That which is flesh is flesh,
no matter whether it is cultivated flesh,
or ignorant flesh or common, ordinary flesh.
That which is flesh is flesh,
and all your lodges,
all your money on God Almighty's earth
can never change your nature.
Never. That's got to come
by and through repentance and faith
in Jesus Christ.
That's the only way you will ever get it changed.
We have more people with fool ways
trying to get into heaven,
and there's only one way to do it
and that is by and through repentance and faith
in Jesus Christ.

Billy Sunday

Remember not the events of the past,
the things of long ago consider not;
See, I am doing something new!
Now it springs forth,
do you not perceive it?
In the desert I make a way,
in the wasteland, rivers . . .
It is I, I, who wipe out,
for my own sake, your offenses;
your sins I remember no more.

Isaiah 43:18–19, 25

Whatever promises God has made
have been fulfilled in him;
therefore it is through him
that we address our Amen to God
when we worship together.
God is the one who firmly establishes us
along with you in Christ;
it is he who anointed us
and has sealed us,
thereby depositing the first payment,
the Spirit in our hearts.

2 Corinthians 1:20–22

When Jesus saw their faith,
he said to the paralyzed man,
"My son, your sins are forgiven."
Now some of the scribes were sitting there
asking themselves: "Why does the man
talk in that way? He commits blasphemy!
Who can forgive sins except God alone?"
Jesus was immediately aware of their reasoning,
though they kept it to themselves,
and he said to them:
"Why do you harbor these thoughts?
Which is easier, to say to the paralytic,
'Your sins are forgiven' or to say,
'Stand up, pick up your mat, and walk again'?
That you may know that the Son of Man
has authority on earth to forgive sins"
(he said to the paralyzed man),

"I command you: Stand up!
Pick up your mat and go home."
The man stood and picked up his mat
and went outside in the sight of everyone.
They were awestruck;
all gave praise to God, saying,
"We have never seen anything like this!"

                              Mark 2:5–12

We had thought to escape by our own power
from the strangling anxiety
of being frail and transitory.
We had hoped by a thousand different methods
of our own clever devising
to run away from our own being,
and thus become masters of an eternal existence.
But bitter experience has taught us
that we cannot help ourselves,
that we are powerless to redeem ourselves
from ourselves.
And so we have called upon
your reality and your truth;
we have called down upon ourselves
the plenitude of your life.
We have made appeal
to your wisdom and your justice,
your goodness and your mercy.
We have summoned you,
so that you yourself might come
and tear down the barriers of our finiteness,
and turn our poverty into riches,
our temporality into eternity.

                              Karl Rahner

The Wedding Feast

Thus says the Lord:
I will lead her into the desert
and speak to her heart.
She shall respond there
as in the days of her youth,
when she came up from the land of Egypt.
I will espouse you to me forever;
I will espouse you in right and in justice,
in love and in mercy;
I will espouse you in fidelity,
and you shall know the Lord.

Hosea 2:14–15, 19–20

The fact of Jesus' friendship
can never be doubted.
It is confirmed
by the extraordinary devotion,
literally unto death,
which the disciples later displayed.
The main support
for this argument is Paul,
who knew Jesus only after death,
yet whose attitude
toward the risen Christ
must be termed
a diffident yet deeply felt
friendship:
he tells him his complaints,
his objections, his feelings,
as he never does to God the Father . . .

Paul would never have dared
display such affection
had he not heard,
understood or felt
that the apostles were
on an intimate footing
with the Lord.
                    Flor Hofmans

People came to Jesus with the objection,
"Why do John's disciples
and those of the Pharisees fast
while yours do not?"
Jesus replied: "How can
the guests at a wedding fast
as long as the groom is still among them?
So long as the groom stays with them,
they cannot fast."
                    Mark 2:18–19

157

Jesus lived with his disciples
almost always in the open air.
Sometimes he got into a boat,
and instructed his hearers,
who were crowded upon the shore.
Sometimes he sat upon the mountains
which bordered the lake,
where the air is so pure
and the horizon so luminous.
The faithful band led thus
a joyous and wandering life,
gathering the inspirations of the master
in their first bloom.
An innocent doubt was sometimes raised,
a question slightly skeptical
but Jesus, with a smile or a look,
silenced the objection.
At each step—
in the passing cloud,
the germinating seed,
the ripening corn—
they saw the sign of the kingdom
drawing nigh,
they believed themselves
on the eve of seeing God,
of being masters of the world;
tears were turned into joy;
it was the advent upon earth
of universal consolation.

                                    Ernest Renan

This great confidence in God is ours,
through Christ.
It is not that we are entitled of ourselves
to take credit for anything.
Our sole credit is from God,
who has made us qualified ministers
of a new covenant,
a covenant not of a written law but of spirit.
The written law kills,
but the Spirit gives life.

2 Corinthians 3:4–6

Master of the Sabbath

It is because God is beautiful
that things are beautiful;
because he is good
that they are good;
because he is
that they are.

St. Augustine

The greatest prayers of men
have always been prayers for light and love.
We cannot buy light and love
in the market place of men;
but they are given to us
'without money and without price.'

Juan Mascaro

God, who said, "Let light shine out of darkness,"
has shone in our hearts,
that we in turn might make known the glory of God
shining on the face of Christ.

2 Corinthians 4:6

"Take care to keep holy the sabbath day
as the Lord, your God, commanded you . . .
For remember that you too
were once slaves in Egypt,
and the Lord, your God,
brought you from there
with his strong hand and outstretched arm.
That is why the Lord, your God,
has commanded you
to observe the sabbath day."

Deuteronomy 5:12, 15

Jesus returned to the synagogue where there was a man whose hand was shriveled up. They kept an eye on Jesus to see whether he would heal him on the sabbath, hoping to be able to bring an accusation against him.

He addressed the man with the shriveled hand: "Stand up here in front!" Then he said to them: "Is it permitted to do a good deed on the sabbath—or an evil one? To preserve life—or to destroy it?"

At this they remained silent. He looked around at them angrily, for he was deeply grieved that they had closed their minds against him.

Then he said to the man, "Stretch out your hand." The man did so and his hand was perfectly restored.

When the Pharisees went outside, they immediately began to plot with the Herodians on how they might destroy him.

Mark 3:1–6

Satan Defeated

In Christ, the new free man,
God promised and revealed and created
the way to a new and true freedom.
Sinful man thinks he can find freedom
by self-confidently controlling himself
and his own life.
But he is warned
that he can only win freedom
by abdicating this control to another—
not to men, who would reduce him
to the rank of a slave,
but to God, who will accept him as his child.
To be able to do what one wants
is only the appearance of freedom;
true freedom is to will what God does.

Hans Küng

The scribes who arrived from Jerusalem
asserted, "He is possessed by Beelzebul,"
and "He expels demons
with the help of the prince of demons."
Summoning them, he then began
to speak to them by way of examples:
"How can Satan expel Satan?
If a kingdom is torn by civil strife,
that kingdom cannot last.
If a household is divided

according to loyalties,
that household will not survive.
Similarly, if Satan has suffered mutiny
in his ranks and is torn by dissension,
he cannot endure;
he is finished.
No one can enter a strong man's house
and despoil his property
unless he has first put him under restraint.
Only then can he plunder his house."

Mark 3:22–27

We do not lose heart
because our inner being
is renewed each day,
even though our body
is being destroyed at the same time.
The present burden of our trial
is light enough and earns for us
an eternal weight of glory
beyond all comparison.
We do not fix our gaze
on what is seen
but on what is unseen.
What is seen is transitory;
what is not seen lasts forever.
Indeed, we know that when the earthly tent
in which we dwell is destroyed
we have a dwelling provided for us
by God, a dwelling in the heavens,
not made by hands, but to last forever.

2 Corinthians 4:16–18—5:1

After Adam had eaten of the tree
the Lord God called him
and asked him, "Where are you?"
He answered, "I heard you in the garden;
but I was afraid, because I was naked,
so I hid myself."
Then he asked, "Who told you that you were naked?
You have eaten, then, from the tree
of which I had forbidden you to eat!"
The man replied,
"The woman whom you put here with me—
she gave me fruit from the tree,
and so I ate it."
The Lord God then asked the woman,
"Why did you do such a thing?"
The woman answered,
"The serpent tricked me into it, so I ate it."

Genesis 3:9–13

It is so hard to be always good,
it is so difficult always to resist
the temptations that surround us on all sides,
it is far from easy to accept cheerfully
the trials of life, which, we can argue,
do not come from God but from wicked men.
All this is perfectly true,
for the fact is that human nature is not able
to live the Christian life by itself alone.
It was never intended to do so,
and for that reason Christ,
who knew all our weaknesses,
and foresaw all our needs,
has arranged that his divine grace
would be ever in his Church
within our reach every day
and every moment of our lives.

Kevin O'Sullivan

The Growth of the Kingdom

The resurrection is the resurrection of the body;
but not the separate body of the individual,
but the body of mankind as one body.
The fall of man is the fall
into division of the human race,
the dismemberment of the first man, Adam;
and the resurrection or rebirth
through the second man, Christ,
is to reconstitute the lost unity . . .
till we all come to one perfect man.

                                    Norman O. Brown

"What comparison shall we use
for the reign of God?
What image will help to present it?
It is like mustard seed
which, when planted in the soil
is the smallest of all the earth's seeds,
yet once it is sown,
springs up to become the largest of shrubs,
with branches big enough
for the birds of the sky
to build nests in its shade."

                                    Mark 4:30–32

I, too, will take from the crest of the cedar,
from its topmost branches
tear off a tender shoot,
and plant it on a high and lofty mountain;
on the mountain heights of Israel
I will plant it.
It shall put forth branches and bear fruit,
and become a majestic cedar.
Birds of every kind shall dwell beneath it,
every winged thing in the shade of its boughs.
Ezekiel 17:22–23

We make it our aim to please him
whether we are with him or away from him.
The lives of all of us
are to be revealed
before the tribunal of Christ
so that each one may receive
his recompense, good or bad,
according to his life in the body.

2 Corinthians 5:9–10

Revelation speaks not only
of a continued life of the soul
but of the resurrection of the body as well.
It is not to be realized
immediately after death
but is promised at the end of time.
This is not an empty promise
but the word of God;
the resurrection of Christ
is its first fulfillment and guarantee
for its realization in us.
We are promised a life
in which we can enjoy forever
all the values of a bodily existence
without having to endure
all of the inadequacies
and drudgery of the present.

Norbert M. Luyten

THE
CHURCH
IN
SUMMER

The Lord's Strength

The love of Christ impels us
who have reached the conviction
that since one died for all, all died.
He died for all so that those who live
might live no longer for themselves,
but for him who for their sakes
died and was raised up.
Because of this we no longer look on anyone
in terms of mere human judgment . . .
This means that if anyone is in Christ,
he is a new creation.
The old order has passed away;
now all is new!

2 Corinthians 5:14–17

The Lord addressed Job
out of the storm and said:
Who shut within doors the sea,
when it burst forth from the womb;
When I made the clouds its garment
and thick darkness its swaddling bands?
When I set limits for it
and fastened the bar of its door,
And said: Thus far shall you come
but no farther,
and here shall your proud waves be stilled!

Job 38:1, 8–11

And they remembered that God was their strength.

Dag Hammarskjöld

The waves were breaking over the boat
and it began to ship water badly.
Jesus was in the stern through it all,
sound asleep on a cushion.
They finally woke him and said to him,
"Teacher, doesn't it matter to you
that we are going to drown?"
He awoke and rebuked the wind
and said to the sea: "Quiet! Be still!"
The wind fell off and everything grew calm.
Then he said to them,
"Why are you so terrified?
Why are you lacking in faith?"
A great awe overcame them at this.
They kept saying to one another,
"Who can this be
that the wind and the sea obey him?"

Mark 4:37–41

The practice of faith and courage begins
with the small details of daily life.
The first step is to notice
where and when one loses faith,
to look through the rationalizations
which are used to cover up this loss of faith,
to recognize where one acts in a cowardly way,
and again how one rationalizes it . . .
Then one will also recognize
that while one is consciously afraid
of not being loved,
the real, though usually unconscious fear,
is that of loving.
To love means to commit oneself
without guarantee,
to give oneself completely in the hope

that our love will produce love
in the loved person.
Love is an act of faith,
and whoever is of little faith
is also of little love.

Erich Fromm

Jesus was a remarkably well balanced man.
Well balanced physically, for a start;
the man whom we see in action
continuously for two and a half years,
walking long distances in every weather,
speaking to big audiences in the open air,
withstanding the fatigue
caused by the continual proximity of followers,
the inquisitive and beggars,
was obviously a solid, healthy man,
as we should expect
a countryman of thirty to be.
He was also certainly well balanced mentally;
one would be almost ashamed to make the point
if self-styled critics had not spoken
of "the madness of Jesus,"
and if psychiatrists had not visualized him
as schizophrenic or paranoiac,
although everything we know about him
reveals a sense of reality and proportion
which gives the lie to these absurd theories.
We must be grateful to Renan
for disposing of them so contemptuously:
"The madman never succeeds.
So far it has not been granted
to a wandering mind
to exert any serious effect
on the progress of humanity."

Henri Daniel-Rops

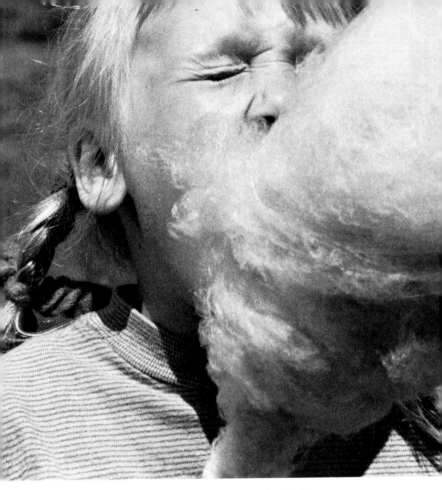

The Life of the World

God did not make death,
nor does he rejoice
in the destruction of the living.
For he fashioned all things
that they might have being;
and the creatures of the world
are wholesome.
                    Wisdom 1:13–14

People from the official's house
arrived saying, "Your daughter is dead.
Why bother the Teacher further?"
Jesus disregarded the report
that had been brought and said to the official:
"Fear is useless. What is needed is trust." . . .
Jesus took the child's father and mother
and his own companions
and entered the room where the child lay.
Taking her hand he said to her,
"Talitha, koum," which means,
"Little girl, get up."
The girl, a child of twelve,
stood up immediately and began to walk around.
At this the family's astonishment was complete.
He enjoined them strictly
not to let anyone know about it,
and told them to give her something to eat.

                               Mark 5:35–36, 40–43

You are well acquainted with the favor
shown you by our Lord Jesus Christ:
how for your sake he made himself poor
though he was rich,
so that you might become rich
by his poverty.
The relief of others
ought not to impoverish you;
there should be a certain equality.
Your plenty at the present time
should supply their need
so that their surplus may in turn
one day supply your need,
with equality as the result.

                          2 Corinthians 8:9, 13–14

The man of faith
is always the man of tomorrow.
He suffers today but he knows
he shall be healed tomorrow.
He dies at the hands of the blind
but he knows that tomorrow
their blindness shall be taken from them
and that they too shall live.

Anthony T. Padovano

I am certain about immortality
at the high points of my life
and it accompanies me in my everyday life.
Immortality is not of my knowledge
but of my love. It exists
as the faithfulness of my action,
as dependability.

This consciousness of immortality
needs no knowledge,
no guarantee, no threat.
It lies in love,
in this marvelous reality
in which we are given to ourselves.
We are mortal when we are without love
and immortal when we love.

Karl Jaspers

A Rebellious People

The very word revelation,
the act of revealing,
means disclosure of the hidden and obscure.
Therefore, revelation offers assistance
where human reason confronts
insoluble problems,
where our seeking gets lost in the dark
or stumbles on relationships
it cannot explain.
God's word brings solution and insight
precisely where our fate
is most difficult to bear,
where we have the bitterest struggles
with unanswered questions.

                              Norbert M. Luyten

Jesus went to his own part of the country
followed by his disciples.
When the sabbath came
he began to teach in the synagogue
in a way that kept his large audience
amazed. They said:
"Where did he get all this?
What kind of wisdom is he endowed with?
How is it such miraculous deeds
are accomplished by his hands?
Isn't this the carpenter, the son of Mary,
a brother of James and Joses
and Judas and Simon?
Aren't his sisters our neighbors here?"
They found him too much for them.

                              Mark 6:1–3

The Spirit entered into me and set me on my feet,
and I heard the one who was speaking
say to me: Son of man,
I am sending you to the Israelites,
rebels who have rebelled against me . . .
But you shall say to them:
Thus says the Lord God!
And whether they heed or resist—
for they are a rebellious house—
they shall know that a prophet has been among them.
                                                    Ezekiel 2:2–5

As to the extraordinary revelations,
in order that I might not become conceited
I was given a thorn in the flesh,
an angel of Satan to beat me
and keep me from getting proud.
Three times I begged the Lord
that this might leave me.
He said to me,
"My grace is enough for you
for in weakness
power reaches perfection."
And so I willingly boast
of my weaknesses instead,
that the power of Christ
may rest upon me.

2 Corinthians 12:7–9

In the messianic time of salvation,
according to the prophetic expectation of salvation,
not only individual prophets and wise men,
warriors, singers and kings,
were to be fulfilled by the spirit of God,
by God's creating power and strength of life;
it was to be given to the whole people.

Hans Küng

Sent out to Preach

Prayer reaches our lives
as we begin to do things
we could not have done
unless we had prayed.
We begin to believe,
we seek forgiveness,
we love those who would otherwise
have been unlovable to us,
we attend to the important things in life.
Prayer is not a pious addition
to things we would have done anyway.
It is a force allowing things to happen
which could not have occurred without it.
Jesus could not have gone to the cross
unless he had first prayed in Gethsemane.
Anthony T. Padovano

It is in Christ and through his blood
that we have been redeemed
and our sins forgiven,
so immeasurably generous
is God's favor to us.
God has given us the wisdom
to understand fully the mystery,
the plan he was pleased to decree in Christ,
to be carried out in the fullness of time:
namely, to bring all things
in the heavens and on earth
into one under Christ's headship.
Ephesians 1:7–10

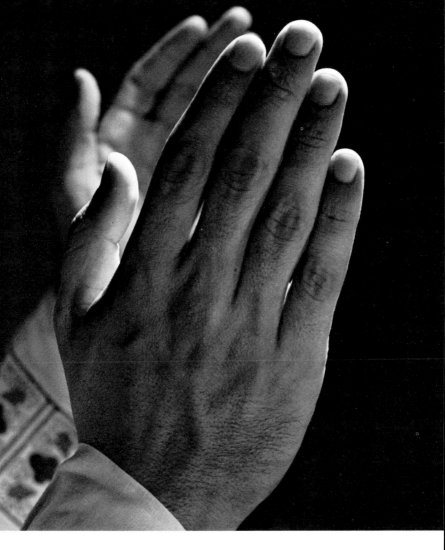

Amos answered Amaziah,
"I was no prophet, nor have I
belonged to a company of prophets;
I was a shepherd and a dresser of sycamores.
The Lord took me from following the flock,
and said to me, Go, prophesy
to my people Israel."

Amos 7:14–15

Jesus summoned the Twelve
and began to send them out two by two,
giving them authority over unclean spirits . . .
"Whatever house you find yourself in,
stay there until you leave the locality.
If any place will not receive you or hear you,
shake its dust from your feet
in testimony against them as you leave."
With that they went off,
preaching the need of repentance.
They expelled many demons,
anointed the sick with oil,
and worked many cures.

Mark 6:7, 10–13

It is not sins that will keep us from heaven,
but the refusal to repent of them.

Kevin O'Sullivan

Shepherd of the Flock

I myself will gather the remnant of my flock
from all the lands to which I have driven them
and bring them back to their meadow;
there they shall increase and multiply.
I will appoint shepherds for them
who will shepherd them so that they
need no longer fear and tremble;
and none shall be missing, says the Lord.

Jeremiah 23:3–4

The only promise for the future of the Church
is that it will be a preaching and a believing Church.
Apart from that, there is nothing ahead for it.
But being given that,
there is nothing which need daunt it,
for its very tribulations will be signs of splendor,
and its struggles will be tokens
that God had girded it with glory.
And we shall have advanced
as far as we can ourselves advance
toward the glory of the Church to come
when we have bowed our heads
and recognized that not we, but only God—
that not our words, but only God's Word—
can make a Church.
What we have today in the shape of a Church
is perhaps hardly worth maintaining.
But we do not need to worry about maintaining this,
for at every breath of the Gospel preached,
the Church comes alive,
and stands on its own feet,
and makes itself a name.

Norman F. Langford

People were coming and going in great numbers,
making it impossible for them to so much as eat.
So Jesus and the apostles went off
in the boat by themselves to a deserted place.
People saw them leaving,
and many got to know about it.
People from all the towns hastened on foot
to the place, arriving ahead of them.
Upon disembarking Jesus saw a vast crowd.
He pitied them,
for they were like sheep without a shepherd;
and he began to teach them at great length.

Mark 6:31–34

In Christ Jesus you who once were far off
have been brought near
through the blood of Christ.
It is he who is our peace,
and who made the two of us one
by breaking down the barrier of hostility
that kept us apart.
In his own flesh he abolished the law
with its commands and precepts,
to create in himself one new man
from us who had been two,
and to make peace,
reconciling both of us to God
in one body through his cross
which put that enmity to death.

Ephesians 2:13–16

With the advantage of hindsight,
we can see how significant it is
that Christ did not employ the concept of remnant,
but used, instead, the utterly different idea of leaven.
Superficially, the two ideas are similar,
since both refer to what is small,
but they lead in opposite directions.
A people trying to be a remnant,
keeping itself pure and undefiled
in the midst of a wicked world,
may reveal a certain nobility of character,
but it is radically different
from the pattern taught by Christ.
The wonder of leaven
is that it is effective,
not by keeping itself separate from the world,
but rather by *penetrating* the world.

Elton Trueblood

Food for the People

Make every effort to preserve the unity
which has the Spirit as its origin
and peace as its binding force.
There is but one body and one Spirit,
just as there is but one hope
given all of you by your call.
There is one Lord,
one faith, one baptism;
one God and Father of all,
who is over all,
and works through all,
and is in all.

Ephesians 4:3–6

Our Savior, when about to depart
out of this world to the Father,
instituted this sacrament,
in which he poured forth, as it were,
the riches of his divine love towards men,
making a remembrance of his wonderful works;
and he commanded us in the participation thereof,
to venerate his memory
and to show forth his death
until he come to judge the world.
And he willed also that this sacrament
should be received as the spiritual food of souls,
whereby may be fed and strengthened
those who live with his life, who said:
"He that eateth me,
the same also shall live by me." (John 6:58) . . .
He willed furthermore that it should be

a pledge of our glory to come,
and of everlasting happiness,
and thus be a symbol of that one body,
whereof he is the head,
and to which he would fain
have us as members be united
by the closest bonds of faith, hope, and charity,
"that we might all speak the same things,
and there might be no schisms amongst us."

Council of Trent

Three times, at least, Jesus took food,
and charged it with a special significance.
Three times he took the things
men eat in this world,
and with a word of blessing transported them
into the presence of another world.
Once he did it to show
that the grace of God is sufficient
for all men's needs.
Another time he did it as a sign
that by his death
many would be redeemed from their sins.
This third time he made use of a simple meal
to overwhelm the disciples
with the truth that there is no more death.

Norman F. Langford

A man came . . . bringing to Elisha,
the man of God,
twenty barley loaves made from the first fruits
and fresh grain in the ear.
"Give it to the people to eat," Elisha said.
But his servant objected, "How can I
set this before a hundred men?"
"Give it to the people to eat," Elisha insisted.
"For thus says the Lord,
'They shall eat
and there shall be some left over.' "
And when they had eaten,
there was some left over,
as the Lord had said.

                2 Kings 4:42–44

Jesus then took the loaves of bread,
gave thanks, and passed them around
to those reclining there;
he did the same with the dried fish,
as much as they wanted.
When they had had enough,
he told his disciples,
"Gather up the crusts that are left over
so that nothing will go to waste."
At this, they gathered twelve baskets
full of pieces left over
by those who had been fed
with the five barley loaves.
When the people saw the sign
he had performed
they began to say,
"This is undoubtedly the Prophet
who is to come into the world."

                John 6:11–14

The Hunger for Life

Not by meditation and reflection
does one grasp the great secret
which hovers over the world and human life.
The higher realization flowers
only in work and action.
For this highest realization
there is no difference
between the wise and the simple.
The simple, if they act,
are given insights
kept from the wise.

Albert Schweitzer

Then the Lord said to Moses,
"I will now rain down
bread from heaven for you.
Each day the people are to go out
and gather their daily portion;
thus will I test them,
to see whether they follow
my instructions or not.
I have heard the grumbling of the Israelites.
Tell them: In the evening twilight
you shall eat flesh,
and in the morning
you shall have your fill of bread,
so that you may know that I,
the Lord, am your God."

Exodus 16:4, 12

You must lay aside your former way of life
and the old self which deteriorates
through illusion and desire,
and acquire a fresh,
spiritual way of thinking.
You must put on that new man
created in God's image,
whose justice and holiness
are born of truth.

Ephesians 4:22–24

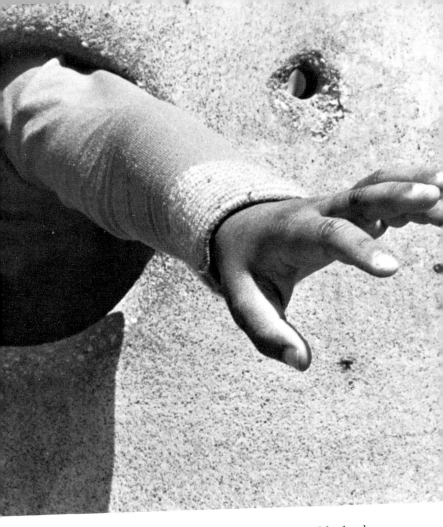

"You should not be working for perishable food
but for food that remains unto life eternal,
food which the Son of Man will give you . . .
I myself am the bread of life.
No one who comes to me
shall ever be hungry,
no one who believes in me
shall thirst again."

John 6:27, 35

He even felt he could smell his freedom, pine-scented, coming out of the woods, until the old man would continue, "You were born into bondage and baptized into freedom, into the death of the Lord, into the death of the Lord Jesus Christ."

Then the child would feel a sullenness creeping over him, a slow warm rising resentment that this freedom had to be connected with Jesus and that Jesus had to be the Lord.

"Jesus is the bread of life," the old man said.

The boy, disconcerted, would look off into the distance over the dark blue treeline where the world stretched out, hidden and at its ease. In the darkest, most private part of his soul, hanging upsidedown like a sleeping bat, was the certain undeniable knowledge that he was not hungry for the bread of life. Had the bush flamed for Moses, the sun stood still for Joshua, the lions turned aside before Daniel only to prophesy the bread of life? Jesus? He felt a terrible disappointment in that conclusion, a dread that it was true. The old man said that as soon as he died, he would hasten to the banks of the Lake of Galilee to eat the loaves and fishes that the Lord had multiplied.

"Forever?" the horrified boy asked.

"Forever," the old man said.

The boy sensed that this was the heart of his great-uncle's madness, this hunger, and what he was secretly afraid of was that it might be passed down, might be hidden in the blood and might strike some day in him and then he would be torn by hunger like the old man, the bottom split out of his stomach so that nothing would heal or fill it but the bread of life.

The Violent Bear It Away
Flannery O'Connor

The Spirit Who Fulfills

The Spirit is thus the earthly presence
of the glorified Lord.
In the Spirit
Christ becomes Lord of his Church,
and in the Spirit
the resurrected Lord acts
both in the community and in the individual.
The power of his resurrection is more
than a power of ecstasy and miracle;
it produces a new creation.
The Spirit opens up for the believer
the way to the saving action of God in Christ.
He does this not as a magic power
which man cannot resist;
he creates the possibility of man's replying
with a responsible and conscious affirmative.
He gives him, through the knowledge
of the crucified Christ,
the realization that in Jesus Christ
God acted for him.
The Spirit gives faith
in the cross and resurrection of Christ
and gives the power to live a life of faith.

Hans Küng

"No one can come to me
unless the Father who sent me draws him;
I will raise him up on the last day.
It is written in the prophets:
'They shall all be taught by God.'
Everyone who has heard the Father
and learned from him
comes to me."

John 6:44–45

Elijah went a day's journey into the desert,
until he came to a broom tree
and sat beneath it.
He prayed for death:
"This is enough, O Lord! Take my life,
for I am no better than my fathers."
He lay down and fell asleep
under the broom tree,
but then an angel touched him
and ordered him to get up and eat.
He looked and there at his head
was a hearth cake and a jug of water.
After he ate and drank,
he lay down again,
but the angel of the Lord came back a second time,
touched him, and ordered,
"Get up and eat,
else the journey will be too long for you!"
He got up, ate and drank;
then strengthened by that food,
he walked forty days and forty nights
to the mountain of God, Horeb.

I Kings 19:4–8

The meaning of this life for the believer
is never accomplished in pure immanence
but always directs him beyond
to a transcendent world.
Therefore, death is never ultimate collapse
but transition to a transcendent world
that has always been present.
It is not ultimate failure
but ultimate fulfillment;
not hopeless absurdity
but the definitive revelation
of life's meaning.

Norbert M. Luyten

Do nothing to sadden the Holy Spirit
with whom you were sealed
against the day of redemption.
Get rid of all bitterness,
all passion and anger,
harsh words, slander,
and malice of every kind.
In place of these,
be kind to one another,
compassionate,
and mutually forgiving,
just as God
has forgiven you in Christ.

Ephesians 4:30–32

Wisdom's Table

Be filled with the Spirit,
addressing one another in psalms
and hymns and inspired songs.
Sing praise to the Lord
with all your hearts.
Give thanks to God the Father
always and for everything
in the name of our Lord Jesus Christ.
                              Ephesians 5:18–20

I rejoice to be here.
It is that old transfiguring impulse.
God is at it again.
Look at you! You are alive!
Indeed you are a kind of glory!
Look at me! Laughing yet!
This is no mountaintop,
we know that for sure.
It is not time for pitching tents
or settling down.
It is time, at once,
for silence, song,
sitting still and moving on.
The world and our way of being in it are good.
For now that is all we know
or need to know of God.
                              James Carroll

He comes to the thought of those
who know him beyond thought,
not to those who imagine
he can be attained by thought:
he is unknown to the learned
and known to the simple.

Kena Upanishad

Wisdom has built her house,
she has set up her seven columns;
She has dressed her meat,
mixed her wine,
yes, she has spread her table.
She has sent out her maidens; she calls
from the heights out over the city:
"Let whoever is simple turn in here;
to him who lacks understanding, I say,
Come, eat of my food,
and drink of the wine I have mixed!
Forsake foolishness that you may live;
advance in the way of understanding."

Proverbs 9:1–6

"I myself am the living bread
come down from heaven.
If anyone eats this bread
he shall live forever;
the bread I will give
is my flesh, for the life of the world . . .
For my flesh is real food
and my blood real drink.
The man who feeds on my flesh
and drinks my blood
remains in me, and I in him.
Just as the Father who has life sent me
and I have life because of the Father,
so the man who feeds on me
will have life because of me."

John 6:51, 55–57

Trust in God

Suppose I tried to be satisfied
with what so many today profess
to be the purpose of their lives.
Suppose I defiantly determined to admit my finiteness,
and glory in it alone.
I could only begin to recognize this finiteness
and accept it as my sole destiny,
because I had previously so often stared out
into the vast reaches of limitless space,
to those hazy horizons
where your endless life is just beginning.

Without you, I should founder helplessly
in my own dull and groping narrowness.
I could never feel the pain of longing,
not even deliberately resign myself
to being content with this world,
had not my mind again and again soared out
over its own limitations into the hushed reaches
which are filled by you alone,
the silent infinite.
Where should I flee before you,
when all my yearning for the unbounded,
even my bold trust in my littleness,
is really a confession of you?

Karl Rahner

210

After hearing his words,
many of the disciples of Jesus remarked,
"This sort of talk is hard to endure!
How can anyone take it seriously?"
Jesus was fully aware that his disciples
were murmuring in protest
at what he had said.
"Does it shake your faith?" he asked them.
"What, then, if you were to see
the Son of Man ascend
to where he was before . . . ?
It is the spirit that gives life;
the flesh is useless.
The words I spoke to you
are spirit and life.
Yet among you there are some
who do not believe . . .
This is why I have told you
that no one can come to me
unless it is granted him by the Father."

John 6:60–65

When you are present all things are delightful:
but when you are away, all is wearisome.
You create quietness of heart
and great peace and festive joy.
You make us to think well of all things
and in all to praise you:
neither can any thing please long without you;
but if it is to be pleasant and palatable
your grace must be present,
and it must be seasoned
with the seasoning of your wisdom.
If you are sweet, all is sweet:
if you are not sweet: what can please?

Thomas a Kempis

Husbands, love your wives,
as Christ loved the church.
He gave himself up for her
to make her holy,
purifying her in the bath of water
by the power of the word,
to present to himself a glorious church,
holy and immaculate,
without stain or wrinkle
or anything of that sort.
Husbands should love their wives
as they do their own bodies.
He who loves his wife loves himself.
Observe that no one ever hates his own flesh;
no, he nourishes it
and takes care of it
as Christ cares for the church—
for we are members of his body.

Ephesians 5:25–30

The people answered,
"Far be it from us to forsake the Lord
for the service of other gods.
For it was the Lord, our God,
who brought us and our fathers
up out of the land of Egypt,
out of a state of slavery.
He performed those great miracles
before our very eyes
and protected us along our entire journey
and among all the peoples
through whom we passed.
Therefore we also will serve the Lord,
for he is our God."

Joshua 24:16–18

The Clean of Heart

"Now, Israel,
hear the statutes and decrees
which I am teaching you to observe,
that you may live, and may enter in
and take possession of the land
which the Lord, the God of your fathers,
is giving you.
In your observance of the commandments
of the Lord, your God,
which I enjoin upon you,
you shall not add
to what I command you
nor subtract from it.
Observe them carefully
for thus will you give evidence
of your wisdom and intelligence
to the nations, who will hear
of all these statutes and say,
'This great nation is truly
a wise and intelligent people.' "
Deuteronomy 4:1–2, 6

We may no longer believe in the doctrine of
tit for tat; we may not meet hatred by hatred,
violence by violence, evil by evil; but we
have to make a continuous and persistent
effort to return good for evil.
Mohandas Gandhi

214

Let one therefore keep the mind pure,
for what a man thinks that he becomes:
this is a mystery of Eternity.

Maitri Upanishad

Jesus summoned the crowd again
and said to them: "Hear me,
all of you, and try to understand.
Nothing that enters a man from outside
can make him impure;
that which comes out of him,
and only that,
constitutes impurity.
Let everyone heed what he hears!
Wicked designs come
from the deep recesses of the heart:
acts of fornication, theft, murder,
adulterous conduct, greed,
maliciousness, deceit, sensuality,
envy, blasphemy, arrogance,
an obtuse spirit.
All these evils come from within
and render a man impure."

                    Mark 7:14–16, 21–23

He wills to bring us to birth
with a word spoken in truth
so that we may be a kind of firstfruits
of his creatures.
Humbly welcome the word
that has taken root in you,
with its power to save you.
Act on this word.
If all you do is listen to it,
you are deceiving yourselves.

                    James 1:17–18, 21–22

Here Is Your God

The Christian community comes into being
through the inspiration of the Spirit of God
and it is cemented together by the Word of God.
All members of the community owe obedience
to the Spirit and the Word.
The fruit of this obedience is the community.

Yet this is not all. In the community
the same divine intention and force operate
that brought about the Incarnation—
the coming of God into this world
to heal, redeem, and sanctify all men.
The dedication of Christ to man
is alive in the Christian community;
the community should be dedicated to man.

Ladislas M. Orsy

Say to those whose hearts are frightened:
Be strong, fear not!
Here is your God . . .
he comes to save you.
Then will the eyes of the blind be opened,
the ears of the deaf be cleared;
Then will the lame leap like a stag,
then the tongue of the dumb will sing.
Streams will burst forth in the desert,
and rivers in the steppe.
The burning sands will become pools,
and the thirsty ground, springs of water.

Isaiah 35:4–7

Some people brought him a deaf man
who had a speech impediment
and begged him to lay his hand on him.
Jesus took him off by himself
away from the crowd.
He put his fingers into the man's ears
and, spitting, touched his tongue;
then he looked up to heaven
and emitted a groan.
He said to him "Ephphatha!"
(that is, "Be opened!").
At once the man's ears were opened;
he was freed from the impediment,
and began to speak plainly.
Then he enjoined them strictly
not to tell anyone;
but the more he ordered them not to,
the more they proclaimed it.
Their amazement went beyond all bounds:
"He has done everything well!
He makes the deaf hear and the mute speak!"

Mark 7:32–37

Whoever offers a sacrifice
ought to become a partaker in it,
because the external sacrifice which is offered
is a sign of the interior sacrifice
by which one offers oneself to God.
Hence by the fact
that he partakes in the sacrifice
the offerer shows that he really shares
in the interior sacrifice.

Thomas Aquinas

Jesus was under no illusions
about those for whom he died.
"God commendeth his love toward us,
in that, while we were yet sinners,
Christ died for us."
He died for those who showed
no signs of understanding his sacrifice,
for those who had not really responded to his appeals
and showed no likelihood of doing so,
for those who turned out to have

nothing in common with him.
He died for the completely unpromising,
for those in whose souls his words
and deeds and sacrifice struck no answering chord.

That is the Gospel—that the love of God
was such as to go the limit
for the unpromising and the unresponsive;
such as to shout desperately to the stone deaf
and hold up visions to the blind;
such as to die for those who mocked his death.

Norman F. Langford

Suppose there should come into your assembly
a man fashionably dressed,
with gold rings on his fingers,
and at the same time a poor man
dressed in shabby clothes.
Suppose further you were to take notice
of the well-dressed man and say,
"Sit right here, please;"
whereas you were to say to the poor man,
"You can stand!"
or "Sit over there by my footrest."
Have you not in a case like this
discriminated in your hearts?
Have you not set yourselves up
as judges who hand down corrupt decisions?
Listen, dear brothers,
Did not God choose these who are poor
in the eyes of the world
to be rich in faith
and heirs of the kingdom
he promised to those who love him?

James 2:2–5

THE
CHURCH
IN
AUTUMN

Faith in Action

My brothers, what good is it
to profess faith without practicing it?
Such faith has no power
to save one, has it?
If a brother or sister has nothing to wear
and no food for the day,
and you say to them,
"Good–bye and good luck!
Keep warm and well fed,"
but do not meet their bodily needs,
what good is that?
So it is with the faith
that does nothing in practice.
It is thoroughly lifeless.

James 2:14–17

The Lord God opens my ear
that I may hear
And I have not rebelled,
have not turned back.
I gave my back to those who beat me,
my cheeks to those who plucked my beard;
My face I did not shield
from buffets and spitting.

The Lord God is my help,
therefore I am not disgraced;
I have set my face like flint,
knowing that I shall not be put to shame.

Isaiah 50:5–7

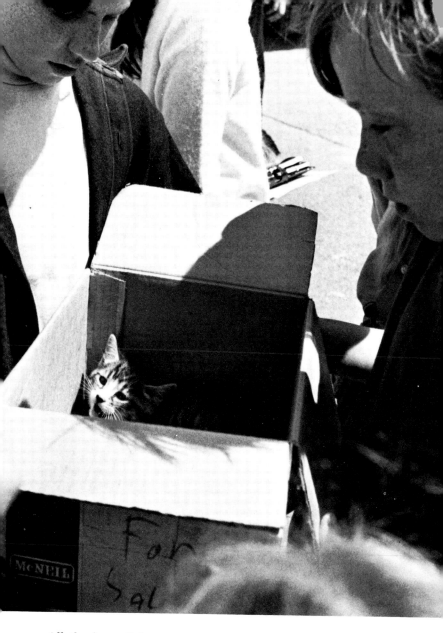

All the beautiful sentiments in the world
weigh less than a single lovely action.
James Russell Lowell

Jesus summoned the crowd with his disciples
and said to them:
"If a man wishes to come after me,
he must deny his very self,
take up his cross,
and follow in my steps.
Whoever would save his life
will lose it,
but whoever loses his life
for my sake and the gospel's
will save it."

Mark 8:34–35

The decisions at which Jesus arrived
in their fundamental principles,
hold good against all lapse of time.
When moral and religious advance is made,
it presents itself as a fresh unfolding
as to what Jesus meant.

C. H. Dodd

About religion.
Did you mean the "study of life"
or Christ's religion?
"Come unto me all you that labor
and are heavy laden
and I will give you rest."
The queer thing is
one does not seem to contradict the other—
one follows the other to me.
If I lose myself in the study of life
and give up *self*
then I am at rest.
But the more I study the religion of Christ
the more I marvel at it.

Katherine Mansfield

The Struggle against Evil

God instructs the heart, not by ideas
but by pains and contradictions.
                                    De Caussade

Jesus and his disciples
came down the mountain
and began to go through Galilee,
but he did not want anyone
to know about it.
He was teaching his disciples
in this vein:
"The Son of Man is going to be delivered
into the hands of men
who will put him to death;
three days after his death he will rise."
Though they failed to understand his words,
they were afraid to question him.

Mark 9:30–32

The wicked say:
Let us beset the just one,
because he is obnoxious to us;
he sets himself against our doings,
Reproaches us for transgressions of the law
and charges us with violations of our training.
Let us see whether his words be true;
let us find out what will happen to him.
For if the just one be the son of God,
he will defend him
and deliver him from the hand of his foes.
With revilement and torture
let us put him to the test
that we may have proof of his gentleness
and try his patience.
Let us condemn him to a shameful death;
for according to his own words,
God will take care of him.

Wisdom 2:12, 17–20

The tragedy of human life does not derive
from the fact that we are corrupt
but from the fact that we often fail to see.
So often we strike down
those who come to us with visions and dreams.
So often we become threatened by an excess of life,
by the sheer power another has to love,
by the grace of another life which confronts us
with our own inadequacy.
Anthony T. Padovano

Where there are jealousy and strife,
there also are inconstancy
and all kinds of vile behavior.
Wisdom from above, by contrast,
is first of all innocent.
It is also peaceable,
lenient, docile, rich in sympathy
and the kindly deeds that are its fruit,
impartial and sincere.
The harvest of justice
is sown in peace
for those who cultivate peace.
James 3:16–18

To struggle against evil,
and to reduce to a minimum
even the ordinary physical evil
which threatens us,
is unquestionably the first act
of our Father who is in heaven;
it would be impossible to conceive him,
and still more impossible to love him,
under any other form.
Pierre Teilhard de Chardin

The Spirit of Jesus

The Spirit of God
is with every man of good will:
he guides them towards God's Kingdom.
Therefore it is important
that we should be able to discern
in our heart and in this world
the signs of the presence and action
of the Holy Spirit
so that we could follow him.

Ladislas M. Orsy

The Lord came down in the cloud and spoke to Moses. Taking some of the spirit that was on him, he bestowed it on the seventy elders; and as the spirit came to rest on them, they prophesied.

Now two men, one named Eldad and the other Medad, were not in the gathering but had been left in the camp. They too had been on the list, but had not gone out to the tent; yet the spirit came to rest on them also, and they prophesied in the camp.

So, when a young man quickly told Moses, "Eldad and Medad are prophesying in the camp." Joshua, son of Nun, who from his youth had been Moses' aide, said, "Moses, my lord, stop them."

But Moses answered him. "Are you jealous for my sake? Would that all the people of the Lord were prophets! Would that the Lord might bestow his spirit on them all!"

Numbers 11:25–29

You rich, weep and wail
over your impending miseries.
Your wealth has rotted,
your fine wardrobe has grown moth–eaten,
your gold and silver have corroded,
and their corrosion shall be
a testimony against you;
it will devour your flesh like a fire.
See what you have stored up
for yourselves against the last days.
Here, crying aloud,
are the wages you withheld
from the farmhands
who harvested your fields.
The shouts of the harvesters have reached
the ears of the Lord of hosts.
You lived in wanton luxury on the earth;
you fattened yourselves for the day of slaughter.
You condemned, even killed, the just man;
he does not resist you.

James 5:1–6

John said to Jesus, "Teacher,
we saw a man using your name
to expel demons
and we tried to stop him
because he is not of our company."
Jesus said in reply:
"Do not try to stop him.
No man who performs a miracle
using my name
can at once speak ill of me.

Anyone who is not against us is with us.
Any man who gives you a drink of water
because you belong to Christ,
will not, I assure you,
go without his reward.
But it would be better
if anyone who leads astray
one of these simple believers
were to be plunged in the sea
with a great millstone
fastened around his neck."

Mark 9:38–42

We hurry from one thing to another;
we exhaust our ingenuity
in devising new amusements
to capture our jaded fancy;
we plunge deeper and deeper
into the mire of self–satisfaction;
and we are further away from peace than ever.
For our hearts are made for God,
and they cannot rest till they rest in him.
He knows our hearts better than we do.
And so in his love, like the Good Shepherd,
he comes to seek us;
he pursues us and he uses his providence
to draw us away from all else,
and to draw all else away from us,
so that we may be driven
to listen to his voice,
and cast ourselves upon his heart.

M. Eugene Boylan

We Are One

In the twentieth century, in this age of fission,
we can split the individual
even as we can split the atom.
Souls, personalities, and egos
are masks, spectres, concealing our unity as body.
For it is as one biological species
that mankind is one . . .
so that to become conscious of ourselves as body
is to become conscious of mankind as one.

Norman O. Brown

The Lord God said:
"It is not good for the man to be alone.
I will make a suitable partner for him."
So the Lord God formed out of the ground
various wild animals and various birds of the air,
and he brought them to the man
to see what he would call them;
whatever the man called each of them
would be its name.
The man gave names to all the cattle,
all the birds of the air,
and all wild animals;
but none proved to be
the suitable partner for the man.
So the Lord God cast
a deep sleep on the man,
and while he was asleep,
he took out one of his ribs
and closed up its place with flesh.
The Lord God then built up into a woman
the rib that he had taken from the man.
When he brought her to the man, the man said:
"This one, at last, is bone of my bones
and flesh of my flesh;
This one shall be called 'woman,'
for out of 'her man' this one has been taken."

Genesis 2:18–23

237

There is one Ruler,
the Spirit that is in all things,
who transforms his own form into many.
Only the wise
who see him in their souls
attain the joy eternal.

Katha Upanishad

Jesus was made for a little while
lower than the angels,
that through God's gracious will
he might taste death
for the sake of all men.
Indeed, it was fitting that,
when bringing many sons to glory,
God, for whom and through whom
all things exist,
should make their leader
in the work of salvation
perfect through suffering.
He who consecrates
and those who are consecrated
have one and the same Father.
Therefore, he is not ashamed
to call them brothers.

Hebrews 2:9–11

People were bringing their little children to him
to have him touch them,
but the disciples were scolding them for this.
Jesus became indignant when he noticed it
and said to them:
"Let the children come to me
and do not hinder them.
It is to just such as these
that the kingdom of God belongs.
I assure you that whoever does not accept
the kingdom of God like a little child
shall not enter into it."
Then he embraced them and blessed them,
placing his hands on them.

Mark 10:13–16

The Knowledge that Transforms

I prayed, and prudence was given me;
I pleaded, and the spirit of Wisdom came to me.
I preferred her to scepter and throne,
And deemed riches nothing
in comparison with her,
nor did I liken any priceless gem to her;
Because all gold, in view of her, is a little sand,
and before her, silver is to be accounted mire.
Beyond health and comeliness I loved her,
And I chose to have her rather than the light,
because the splendor of her never yields to sleep.
Yet all good things together
come to me in her company,
and countless riches at her hands.

Wisdom 7:7–11

How can we approach the heart of all things,
the true heart of reality?
Not by knowledge alone,
but by the full flower of knowledge, love.
Only the experience of knowledge's blooming into love
has any power to work a transformation
in me, in my very self.
For it is only when I am fully present to an object
that I am changed by meeting it.
And it is only in love that I am fully present—
not in bare knowing,
but in the affection engendered by knowing.

Karl Rahner

God's word is living and effective,
sharper than any two–edged sword.
It penetrates and divides soul and spirit,
joints and marrow;
it judges the reflections
and thoughts of the heart.
Nothing is concealed from him;
all lies bare and exposed
to the eyes of him
to whom we must render an account.
Hebrews 4:12–13

Peter was moved to say to him:
"We have put aside everything to follow you!"
Jesus answered: "I give you my word,
there is no one who has given up home,
brothers or sisters, mother or father,
children or property,
for me and for the gospel
who will not receive in this present age
a hundred times as many homes,
brothers and sisters, mothers,
children and property—
and persecution besides—
and in the age to come, everlasting life."
Mark 10:28–30

Providence is not like a script
written beforehand,
nor, as in Hegel,
a process determing events.
It works in and through
the freedom of individual men and women,
and its law is love.
Martin D'Arcy

People believe that *to love* is simple . . .
but that *to be loved* is most difficult . . .
They do not know that the real problem
is not the difficulty of being loved
but the difficulty of loving;
that one is loved only if one can love,
if one's capacity to love
produces love in another person,
that the capacity for love,
not for its counterfeit,
is a most difficult achievement.

                                    Erich Fromm

The Servant of All

Jesus called the Twelve together
and said to them:
"You know how among the Gentiles
those who seem to exercise authority
lord it over them;
their great ones make their importance felt.
It cannot be like that with you.
Anyone among you who aspires to greatness
must serve the rest;
whoever wants to rank first among you
must serve the needs of all.
The Son of Man has not come
to be served but to serve—
to give his life as ransom for the many."
Mark 10:42–45

It is clear that Jesus is not merely concerned
about service at table,
or care for the bodily needs of others,
as suggested by the wider use of the word;
nor is he simply concerned
about certian special acts of love,
which can also be summed up in the word *diakonia*.
His fundamental concern is with living for others;
and the origins of the word *diakonia*,
in contrast to other similar verbs,
indicates that a completely personal service is implied.
This is an essential element in being a disciple:
a man is a disciple of Jesus
through service of his fellow men.
Hans Küng

But who is Jesus? . . .
He is the man for others
against individualistic inwardness.
He is the lonely and forsaken
without transcendent escape.
He worships not in provinciality
but in the midst of real life.
He, though longing for him,
does not experience the *deus ex machina.*
Thus, the time for religion might have gone,
but not the time for Jesus.

Dietrich Bonhoeffer

We have a great high priest
who has passed through the heavens,
Jesus, the Son of God;
let us hold fast to our profession of faith.
For we do not have a high priest
who is unable to sympathize
with our weakness,
but one who was tempted
in every way that we are,
yet never sinned.
So let us confidently approach
the throne of grace
to receive mercy and favor
and to find help in time of need.

Hebrews 4:14–16

Because of his affliction
he shall see the light
in fullness of days;
Through his suffering,
my servant shall justify many,
and their guilt he shall bear.

Isaiah 53:11

246

The Light of Faith

I will gather them
from the ends of the world,
with the blind and the lame in their midst,
The mothers and those with child;
they shall return as an immense throng.
They departed in tears,
but I will console them and guide them;
I will lead them to brooks of water,
on a level road,
so that none shall stumble.

Jeremiah 31:8–9

Every high priest is taken from among men
and made their representative before God,
to offer gifts and sacrifices for sins.
He is able to deal patiently
with erring sinners,
for he is himself beset by weakness
and so must make sin offerings
for himself as well as for the people.
One does not take this honor
on his own initiative,
but only when called by God as Aaron was.
Even Christ did not glorify himself
with the office of the high priest.

Hebrews 5:1–5

As Jesus was leaving Jericho with his disciples
and a sizable crowd,
there was a blind beggar Bartimaeus
("son of Timaeus") sitting by the roadside.
On hearing that it was Jesus of Nazareth,
he began to call out,
"Jesus, Son of David, have pity on me!"
Many people were scolding him
to make him keep quiet,
but he shouted all the louder,
"Son of David, have pity on me!"
Then Jesus stopped and said,
"Call him over."
So they called the blind man over,
telling him as they did so,
"You have nothing whatever to fear from him!
Get up! He is calling you!"
He threw aside his cloak,
jumped up and came to Jesus.
Jesus asked him,
"What do you want me to do for you?"
"Rabboni," the blind man said,
"I want to see."
Jesus said in reply, "Be on your way!
Your faith has healed you."
Immediately he received his sight
and started to follow him up the road.

Mark 10:46–52

The blind Bartimaeus represented what the prophets called blindness, which had nothing to do with the physiological condition of the eyes but was, much more profoundly, a refusal to see, a stubbornness when it came to seeing. Blindness was hard eyes, evil eyes, which saw right through the plight of the poor as though they suddenly were invisible, which saw a representative of God as a troublemaker who should be killed. The blind Bartimaeus was blindness itself coming toward Jesus. He stopped. In those seconds it had taken him to come before Jesus, the entire human situation had been excavated, revealing the shape of charity, the dereliction in being blind and a beggar, and the blindness of everyone standing there watching Bartimaeus. So this representative from the side of blindness met this representative from the side of deliverance. Jesus did *not* first ask him how long he had been blind. Jesus did *not* reach into his purse and extract an especially large gift, which is the very thing he might have done. He instead asked simply, "What do you want me to do for you?" Bartimaeus could not see Jesus, his eyes. But Bartimaeus had grown skilled in listening to voice inflections. He heard no money in the voice, no condescension, no charity. So Bartimaeus lifted up the heaviest words in his vocabulary, trembling with the strain of hoping. The big super–wailer suddenly could do no more than mumble. He had no experience in hoping. He had never said these words to himself, much less out loud and to anyone. But out they came: "Teacher, let me receive my sight." Once said there was no waiting, no dramatic period when Jesus evaluated them, evaluated his worthiness. As soon said, it was done. With a mighty rush from the side of deliverance, the words were spoken with the laughter of pure ecstasy, as Bartimaeus began his laughing with ecstasy, his running around, and shouting, and jumping up into the air, not being able to believe that he could see. He looked, and pointed, and peered, and reveled in color, shapes, gradations, the slants, the roughs, his eyes trying to exhaust the infinite novelty of the total landscape, seeing more in ten seconds than most seeing people see in a lifetime.

John R. Fry

Unconditional Love

Love is not primarily a relationship
to a specific person;
it is an *attitude*, an *orientation* of *character*
which determines the relatedness of a person
to the world as a whole,
not toward one "object" of love.
If a person loves only one other person
and is indifferent to the rest of his fellow men,
his love is not love but a symbiotic attachment,
or an enlarged egotism . . .
If I truly love one person
I love all persons,
I love the world, I love life.
If I can say to somebody else, "I love you,"
I must be able to say, "I love in you everybody,
I love through you the world,
I love in you also myself."

                                    Erich Fromm

Under the old covenant there were many priests
because they were prevented by death
from remaining in office;
but Jesus, because he remains forever,
has a priesthood which does not pass away.
Therefore he is always able to save
those who approach God through him,
since he forever lives
to make intercession for them.

                                    Hebrews 7:23–25

252

Hear, O Israel!
The Lord is our God,
the Lord alone!
Therefore, you shall love
the Lord, your God,
with all your heart,
and with all your soul,
and with all your strength.
Take to heart these words
which I enjoin on you today.

Deuteronomy 6:4–6

Of all the things man can love,
there is at least one which he can love
without limit and unconditionally,
without need for "order" and "moderation,"
and that is you.

In loving your holy immensity, our ordinary life
of enforced moderation and proportion
becomes tolerable.
In you the heart can safely follow
its yearning for the limitless,
can wander aimlessly without going astray.
I can prodigally lavish my affections
on every single aspect of your Being,
and find in each of them everything I seek,
because everything in you is the whole.

Karl Rahner

The scribe said to him:
"Excellent, Teacher! You are right in saying,
'He is the One, there is no other than he.'
Yes, 'to love him with all our heart,
with all our thoughts and with all our strength,
and to love our neighbor as ourselves'
is worth more than any burnt offering
or sacrifice."
Jesus approved the insight of this answer
and told him,
"You are not far from the reign of God."
And no one had the courage
to ask him any more questions.

Mark 12:32–34

The Secret of Giving

But now Jesus has appeared,
at the end of the ages
to take away sins once for all
by his sacrifice.
Just as it is appointed
that men die once,
and after death be judged,
so Christ was offered up once
to take away the sins of many;
he will appear a second time
not to take away sin
but to bring salvation
to those who eagerly await him,
Hebrews 9:26–28

Christ never measured with earthly standards.
He spoke of his own death,
not as the merciless end of his existence,
but rather as a breakthrough
to authentic life in the divine realm.
He taught us how, through him,
we would come to participate
in this divine life that is beyond
all the limits of time.
For, "That is eternal life,
that they know you, Father,
and him whom you sent."
Norbert M. Luyten

Taking a seat opposite the treasury,
Jesus observed the crowd
putting money into the collection box.
Many of the wealthy put in sizable amounts;
but one poor widow came
and put in two small copper coins
worth about a cent.
He called his disciples over
and told them: "I want you
to observe that this poor widow
contributed more than all the others
who donated to the treasury.
They gave from their surplus wealth,
but she gave from her want,
all that she had to live on."

Mark 12:41–44

Elijah the prophet went to Zarephath. As he arrived at the entrance of the city, a widow was gathering sticks there; he called out to her, "Please bring me a small cupful of water to drink." She left to get it, and he called out after her, "Please bring along a bit of bread."

"As the Lord, your God, lives," she answered, "I have nothing baked; there is only a handful of flour in my jar and a little oil in my jug. Just now I was collecting a couple of sticks, to go in and prepare something for myself and my son; when we have eaten it, we shall die."

"Do not be afraid," Elijah said to her. "Go and do as you propose. But first make me a little cake and bring it to me. Then you can prepare something for yourself and your son. For the Lord, the God of Israel, says, 'The jar of flour shall not go empty, nor the jug of oil run dry, until the day when the Lord sends rain upon the earth.'"

She left and did as Elijah said. She was able to eat for a year, and he and her son as well; the jar of flour did not go empty' nor the jug of oil run dry, as the Lord had foretold through Elijah.

I Kings 17:10–16

I pray not for wealth,
I pray not for honors,
I pray not for pleasures,
or even the joys of poetry.
I only pray that during all my life
I may have love:
that I may have pure love to love you.
Chaitanya

The Indescribable Mystery

Jesus said to his disciples:
"During that period after trials of every sort
the sun will be darkened,
the moon will not shed its light,
stars will fall out of the skies,
and the heavenly hosts will be shaken.
Then men will see
the Son of Man coming in the clouds
with great power and glory.
He will dispatch his messengers
and assemble his chosen
from the four winds,
from the farthest bounds of earth and sky . . .
As to the exact day or hour,
no one knows it,
neither the angels in heaven
nor even the Son,
but only the Father."

Mark 13:24–27, 32

At that time your people shall escape,
everyone who is found written in the book.
Many of those who sleep
in the dust of the earth shall awake;
Some shall live forever,
others shall be an everlasting horror and disgrace.
But the wise shall shine brightly
like the splendor of the firmament,
And those who lead the many to justice
shall be like the stars forever.

Daniel 12:1–3

Jesus offered one sacrifice for sins
and took his seat forever
at the right hand of God;
now he waits until his enemies
are placed beneath his feet.
By one offering he has forever perfected
those who are being sanctified.
Once sins have been forgiven,
there is no further offering for sin.

Hebrews 10:12–14

The diction used *about* Christ
has been, and perhaps wisely,
sweet and submissive.
But the diction used by Christ
is quite curiously gigantesque;
It is full of camels leaping through needles
and mountains hurled into the sea.
Morally it is equally terrific;
he called himself a sword of slaughter,
and told men to buy swords
if they sold their coats for them.
That he used other even wilder words
on the side of non-resistance
greatly increased the mystery.

G. K. Chesterton

If the thinker wanted to use the words of the mystic,
he could soon define the nature of God.
God is love and also the end of love:
herein we find the whole contribution of mysticism.
The mystic will never grow tired
of speaking of this twofold love.
His descriptions have no end,
because what he wants to describe
is indescribable.
But he is definite on one point:
that divine love is not something belonging to God:
it is God Himself.

Henri Bergson

The Kingdom of Truth

We have every reason, therefore,
to rejoice in Christ today
and to render him all the gratitude and glory
of which our human nature is capable.
We have the great blessing of being members
of his kingdom after death.
Christ lived and died for us.
He lived to teach us the truth
and show us the way to heaven.
He died to conquer our death
and earn for us eternal life.
He rose from the dead
to prove he had overcome sin and death
and to open the gates of heaven for us.
Christ is "the way, the truth and the life."

Kevin O'Sullivan

As the visions during the night continued,
I saw One like a son of man coming,
on the clouds of heaven;
When he reached the Ancient One
and was presented before him,
He received dominion,
glory, and kingship;
nations and peoples
of every language serve him.
His dominion is an everlasting dominion
that shall not be taken away,
his kingship shall not be destroyed.

Daniel 7:13–14

"My kingdom does not belong to this world.
If my kingdom were of this world,
my subjects would be fighting
to save me from being handed over to the Jews.
As it is my kingdom is not here . . .
The reason I was born,
the reason why I came into the world,
is to testify to the truth.
Anyone committed to the truth
hears my voice."

John 18:36–37

The Israelites were constantly expectant,
and the first Christians too.
Christmas, which might have been thought
to turn our gaze towards the past,
has only fixed it further in the future.
The Messiah who appeared
for a moment in our midst
only allowed himself to be seen
and touched for a moment
before vanishing again,
more luminous and ineffable than ever,
into the depths of the future.
He came. Yet now we must expect him—
no longer a small chosen group among us,
but all men—once again and more than ever.
The Lord Jesus will only come soon
if we ardently expect him.
It is an accumulation of desires
that should cause the Pleroma
to burst upon us.

Pierre Teilhard de Chardin

Jesus Christ is the faithful witness,
the first-born from the dead
and ruler of the kings of earth.
To him who loves us
and freed us from our sins by his own blood,
who has made us
a royal nation of priests
in the service of his God and Father—
to him be glory and power forever and ever!
Amen.

Revelation 1:5–6

Table of Moveable Feasts

Year	Sunday Cycle	Baptism of the Lord	No. of weeks of the year	No. of Sundays after Epiphany	1st Sun. of Lent	Easter	Pentecost	Week after Pentecost corresponds to Week of the Year	Holy Trinity	Sunday after Trinity corresponds to Sunday of the Year of	1st Sun. Advent*
1972	A	Jan. 9	34	6	Feb. 20	Apr. 2	May 21	7	May 28	9	Dec. 3
1973	B	Jan. 7	34	9	Mar. 11	Apr. 22	Jun. 10	10	Jun. 17	12	Dec. 2
1974	C	Jan. 13	33	7	Mar. 3	Apr. 14	Jun. 2	9	Jun. 9	11	Dec. 1
1975	A	Jan. 12	33	5	Feb. 16	Mar. 30	May 18	7	May 25	9	Nov. 30
1976	B	Jan. 11	33	8	Mar. 7	Apr. 18	Jun. 6	10	Jun. 13	12	Nov. 28
1977	C	Jan. 9	33	7	Feb. 27	Apr. 10	May 29	9	Jun. 5	11	Nov. 27
1978	A	Jan. 8	34	5	Feb. 12	Mar. 26	May 14	6	May 21	8	Dec. 3
1979	B	Jan. 7	34	8	Mar. 4	Apr. 15	Jun. 3	9	Jun. 10	11	Dec. 2
1980	C	Jan. 13	33	6	Feb. 24	Apr. 6	May 25	8	Jun. 1	10	Nov. 30

* The Sunday Cycle changes to that of the following year on the First Sunday of Advent, for example, on December 3, 1972 begin Sunday Cycle B.

CONTENTS BY SUNDAYS